Inviting the Spirit into Our Lives

Inviting the Spirit into Our Lives

MAX H. MOLGARD

BOOKCRAFT
Salt Lake City, Utah

Library of Congress Catalog Card Number: 92-76187
ISBN 0-88494-871-4

Second Printing, 1993

Printed in the United States of America

Contents

1

The Invitation

Doug had been waiting for the mailman for almost an hour. "It has to be here today," he thought to himself. "I can't wait until tomorrow. It just has to be here today!"

Doug's mind retreated into the place reserved for daydreams. All of his recent dreams had been reserved for Susan Larson's party. Anybody who was anybody was going to be there. It was the talk at school and at track practice after school. Even the halls of the church on Sunday were filled with the chatter—full of the excitement of anticipation. Several of Doug's friends had already received their invitations. Carma had called him yesterday as soon as she had opened hers. She was surprised that he hadn't received his on the same day. He had promised to call her the minute he received his invitation.

Doug hesitated as the mailman filled his box, then he opened the door and walked double time across the yard. The mailman heard the door slam and turned around to wave. Doug waved with one hand and opened the front of the mailbox with the other. He grabbed the whole bundle and quickly flipped through the mail. He could see the usual junk mail and his mom's *Reader's Digest*. Two bills for his mom and dad, a letter from his missionary brother, Kyle, . . . and there it was, the invitation with Susan Larson's address in the upper left-hand corner!

Doug ran back into the house and threw the rest of the mail on the couch. His heart was pounding so hard that he knew he must be feeling the way Kyle had when he opened his mission call. Doug tore the envelope open, but was careful not to damage the invitation inside. He knew this would be something he wanted to save in what he jokingly called his Treasures of Trash.

Opening the invitation, he read:

THIS IS TO INFORM YOU THAT THE PARTY OF THE CENTURY WILL BE HELD
> DATE: MARCH 25
> TIME: 7:30 p.m.
> PLACE: 335 SO. VISTA
> HOST: SUSAN LARSON

WE GUARANTEE A GOOD TIME WILL BE HAD BY ALL THOSE PRESENT.
> P.S. YOU ARE *NOT* INVITED.

Can you imagine the hurt and disappointment that Doug must have felt when he received this unusual invitation? Our minds explode with questions. How could Susan do such an awful thing? What was she thinking? Why did she not want Doug at her party?

There is, however, a more important question we should ask. Do we ever do the same thing to the Spirit? Do we tell the Spirit that it is not invited into our lives? How could we do such an awful thing? What are we thinking? Why would we not want the Spirit to be with us? These are some serious questions to be considered.

In relating the following experience, President Wilford Woodruff taught the importance of having the Spirit. "Joseph Smith visited me a great deal after his death, and taught me many important principles. . . . Among other things, he told me to get the Spirit of God; that all of us needed it. . . . He said, 'I want you to teach the people to get the Spirit of God. You cannot build up the Kingdom of God without that.' . . ." (*Deseret News* [Weekly], 7 November 1896.)

President Woodruff also stated: "Now, if you have the Holy Ghost with you, . . . I can say unto you that there is no greater gift, there is no greater blessing, there is no greater testimony given to any man on earth. You may have the administration of angels; you may see many miracles; you may see many wonders in the earth; but I claim that the gift of the Holy Ghost is the greatest gift that can be bestowed upon man." (In *Doctrines from the Prophets,* Alma P. Burton, comp. [Salt Lake City: Bookcraft, 1970], p. 229.)

Elder James E. Faust described the benefits of having the Spirit in our lives as follows: "The comforting Spirit of the Holy Ghost can abide with us twenty-four hours a day: when we work, when we play, when we rest. Its strengthening influence can be with us year in and year out. That sustaining influence can be with us in joy and sorrow, when we rejoice as well as when we grieve. The Holy Ghost is the greatest guarantor of inward peace in our unstable world." (*Ensign,* May 1989, p. 32.)

We have all been invited to have the Spirit in our lives. The Lord has repeatedly commanded us to seek the Spirit and follow its counsel. The Holy Ghost leads people to and bears witness of the truthfulness of the gospel. If they act upon this witness by entering into the waters of baptism they will then be given the gift of the Holy Ghost.

The Prophet Joseph Smith explained the difference between the Holy Ghost and the gift of the Holy Ghost as follows:

> There is a difference between the Holy Ghost and the gift of the Holy Ghost. Cornelius received the Holy Ghost before he was baptized, which was the convincing power of God unto him of the truth of the Gospel, but he could not receive the gift of the Holy Ghost until after he was baptized. Had he not taken this sign or ordinance upon him, the Holy Ghost which convinced him of the truth of God, would have left him. (*History of the Church* 4:555.)

The following story illustrates what Joseph Smith was teaching.

As two missionaries were tracting out a neighborhood, they knocked on a door at the end of the last block for the day. A lady answered the door and, after hearing their introductions, made an appointment for them to return the following week.

At the appointed time, the missionaries arrived to find the lady and her husband ready to hear their message. They asked the couple if they knew anything about the Church and its teachings. The lady indicated that she was interested in genealogy and knew the Church had a lot of records, but that was all she knew about the Church.

The missionaries spent the next several weeks teaching the couple. They challenged them to read the Book of Mormon and pray about its truthfulness. They also invited them to attend Church meetings.

The couple began to attend church and study the Book of Mormon. As they prayed about the truthfulness of the Book of Mormon and the Church, they received a witness from the Holy Ghost that it was true.

When the missionaries challenged them to be baptized they said they couldn't because they smoked and were not willing to stop. It wasn't long before they stopped attending Church services and ceased reading the Book of Mormon. Worst of all, they stopped praying. This failure to act upon what the Spirit had told them caused them eventually to lose the warm feeling that had testified to them.

The missionaries began to pray fervently for this couple, asking to be shown how to help them. The answer came to one of the Elders: they should talk to the lady about getting organized. This seemed to be a strange answer, but they acted on the inspiration they felt had been given.

As they visited the couple's home that day, the missionaries told the lady they had been impressed to tell her she should get organized. She responded with the question, "How did you know?" She then admitted that she was so disorganized that it made her nervous, and therefore she smoked. Her disorganization also upset her husband and caused him to smoke.

She went right to work organizing herself. Within two weeks both she and her husband had quit smoking. They again started attending church and reading the Book of Mormon. They were also praying, but this time their prayers were even more sincere. They again felt the warmth of the Spirit, and this time they asked to be baptized.

Some actions or thoughts will keep the Spirit away. For this couple, these consisted of failing to live the Word of Wisdom and refusing to act upon the witness they had received from the Spirit.

On the other hand there are specific things that can help to bring the Spirit into our lives. Attending church, reading the Book of Mormon, and praying—basic to sincere investigation of the gospel—produced that result for this couple.

The principle is very simple. Righteousness invites the Spirit, and unrighteousness drives the Spirit from our lives. Joseph Smith stated: "The Gift of the Holy Ghost by the laying on of hands, cannot be received through the medium of any other principle than the principle of righteousness, for if the proposals are not complied with, it is of no use, but withdraws" (*History of the Church* 3:379).

Living the gospel every day is the number one thing that will invite and maintain the influence of the Spirit in our lives. When we are consistently trying to do this, there are certain things we can do that will bring the Spirit back when temporarily lost to us or will cause an increase in its intensity, while certain other actions, on the other hand, will quickly drive the Spirit from our lives. For literary convenience, in the chapters that follow we consider such actions in isolation, even though in actuality the factors represented as driving out or inviting the Spirit would be related to one's overall spiritual condition.

2

An Invitation Through Love

Laura had been disturbed for a long time by the declared open war that was going on between her mother and her sixteen-year-old brother Jeff. As time had passed, things seemed to grow worse between Jeff and her mother. One of the main bones of contention was a garbage pit in the house called Jeff's bedroom.

Every day, each conversation between Jeff and his mother seemed to be centered around the bedroom. Jeff refused to do anything about the bedroom, and his mother said that she was not going to clean it for him. Jeff always said it was his room and he should be able to leave it dirty if that was what he chose to do. Then he'd ask his mom, "What is a little clutter going to hurt?"

His mom always countered with something like:

"Don't you know that cleanliness is next to godliness?" Or, "How can you bring your friends into this mess?" Or, "What will the neighbors think?" And when those words didn't bring a response, she'd end with, "This is my house and I will not tolerate such a mess!" These conversations invariably ended with the volume being turned to the maximum and Jeff going to his bedroom and slamming the door behind him.

One day Laura came home and heard strange noises coming from Jeff's bedroom. It sounded as if someone was cleaning. She wondered if she was dreaming.

As she looked into the room, she saw her mother cleaning. She asked, "Mother, what in the world are you doing?"

Her mother smiled and answered simply, "Cleaning Jeff's bedroom." Laura was so stunned that she turned around and walked away.

Laura later started to doubt what she had seen; and wondering if it could really be true, she returned to Jeff's bedroom. Her mother was gone, but what she thought she had seen was true. The bedroom was cleaner than it had been for months. As Laura stood looking around the room in amazement, she noticed a piece of paper lying on the bed. She thought her mother must have missed it. Picking up the paper, she found that it was a note from her mother. The note read: "Jeff, I love you! Mom."

When Jeff came home and found the note, a miracle took place. Things were never again the same between Jeff and his mother; the two seemed to get along better each day. (Note to those reading this book who are under the age of twenty-one and still living at home: This story could be reversed. Jeff could have cleaned up his room and left a note reading: "Mom, I love you! Jeff.")

From this story we can see that contention can drive the Spirit from us, but that an infusion of love can quickly provide the environment for inviting the Spirit.

There is probably not one single virtue that can bring the influence of the Holy Ghost more quickly than love. Elder Robert L. Simpson said, "The deepest expression of spirituality is love" (Conference Report, October 1964, p. 94). But on the other hand, there is nothing that drives the Spirit away more quickly than contention. We have all experienced this in our lives. Think how you feel when you are having a heated argument with someone. Whatever feelings of peace, warmth, and light you may have experienced by expressing sincere love, either through word or deed, contention replaces them with feelings of turmoil, bitterness, and darkness. Contention will always drive out the influence of the Holy Ghost.

The principle that love invites the Spirit is demonstrated by the visit of Christ among the people of Nephi. After being introduced by the Father,

> the Lord spake unto them saying: Arise and come forth unto me, that ye may thrust your hands into my side, and also that ye may feel the prints of the nails in my hands and in my feet, that ye may know that I am the God of Israel, and the God of the whole earth, and have been slain for the sins of the world.
>
> And it came to pass that the multitude went forth, and thrust their hands into his side, and did feel the prints of the nails in his hands and in his feet; and this they did do, going forth one by one until they had all gone forth, and did see with their eyes and did feel with their hands, and did know of a surety and did bear record, that it was he, of

whom it was written by the prophets, that should come. (3 Nephi 11:13–15.)

Those who were present that day felt the warmth and peace that can come only from genuine love. Some key words used in this experience are "one by one." Jesus had each person come individually to him to receive a personal, physical witness of his divinity. Words cannot describe what they must have felt that day.

After this experience, which must have lasted several hours, Jesus taught his newly called Twelve how to baptize and gave them power to do so. It is interesting to note that he then talked of the unity of the Godhead and immediately stressed the importance of harmony among Church members:

> And there shall be no disputations among you, as there have hitherto been; neither shall there be disputations among you concerning the points of my doctrine, as there have hitherto been.
>
> For verily, verily I say unto you, he that hath the spirit of contention is not of me, but is of the devil, who is the father of contention, and he stirreth up the hearts of men to contend with anger, one with another.
>
> Behold, this is not my doctrine, to stir up the hearts of men with anger, one against another; but this is my doctrine, that such things should be done away. (3 Nephi 11:28–30.)

We learn, then, that Satan is anchored in contention. This knowledge reveals the real root of Satan's motives. They are based in selfishness and pride. The motives of Heavenly Father and Jesus are based in true love and humility.

Think about the contention we tend to get involved in. What are our real motives? Usually we find they involve a proud heart and selfish desires. Think about Jeff and his mom. Of whom was Jeff thinking? What was his mom thinking about, and whom? What were their real motives? Were their motives based on love and caring?

There is a great difference between the love the world teaches and the love that God teaches. The love the world teaches looks for love in return; in other words, it is conditional—there are always strings attached. The love that God teaches us is unconditional—we are to love others because they are our brothers and sisters, not because of what they do. Notice that Jesus could say of the soldiers while hanging on the cross, "Father, forgive them; for they know not what they do (Luke 23:34).

Conditional love does not invite the Spirit. In many cases it is the very thing that drives the Spirit away. The message that Jeff's mom was giving him in the beginning of the story was, "I love you only if you clean your room." The message she ended up giving him was, "The bedroom is not the issue; the real issue is that I love you."

Unconditional love makes the Spirit welcome in our hearts and can therefore work miracles, as it did with Jeff and his mom. President Thomas S. Monson described this miracle when he spoke of the unconditional love his mother displayed.

At the time of which he was speaking, during the Great Depression, many homeless and unemployed people rode trains around the country. President Monson's family lived close to the railroad tracks, and many of these people would come to the house asking if the Monsons could spare some food. His mother would always invite them in and have them sit at the table while she fed them a sandwich and some pie or cake. She would always ask them about their life, and then she would give them words of encouragement. These visitors were very grateful not only for the food but also for the words of care and love. As a boy Thomas Monson noticed that as they left his home a smile of content had replaced their look of despair. He learned from these visits that unconditional love can work wonders. (See *Ensign,* May 1987, p. 68.)

One of the most basic human needs is the need to be loved. Many studies have been conducted on the impact of love and its effect on us. One of the most interesting studies found that those who are suffering physical pain have less pain when they are surrounded by those who love them. Love brings the Spirit into our lives, and it can be a great comforting influence both physically and spiritually.

The opposite is also true. The lack of love in one's life can have a negative effect, resulting in a loss of the Spirit. President Harold B. Lee related Elder Adam S. Bennion's experience of visiting the Utah State Penitentiary. As he stood before the inmates, Elder Bennion said to them: "Now, I am going to talk with you. I am going to ask you some questions, and I want you to get up and answer me. What was it that brought you here as inmates of this penitentiary? I am frequently a speaker at various gatherings of young people and at graduation exercises, and I would like you to tell me so that I can warn them."

He was able to persuade all the assembled inmates to stand and answer his question. This is what they said, almost without exception: "We are here in the state pentitentiary because there came a time in our lives when we were made to feel that nobody cared what happened to us." (See *New Era,* March 1973, p. 12.)

The giving of unconditional love requires courage and personal commitment, because it can be the cause of some of the greatest suffering we will ever experience. The Savior, our Great Exemplar, suffered the greatest pain ever during the Atonement, an act of profound love in which he opened the door to salvation for all, with no conditions beyond their accepting and following him as their Savior. The following story is a good example of the principle of unconditional love.

Tommy was one of the most difficult students his school had ever encountered. This third-grade boy was cross-eyed, dirty, and smelly. He came to school each day wearing gym shoes tied together with string, and clothes that were soiled and wrinkled. Many students made fun of him with taunts and name-calling.

Tommy's teacher wondered what kind of parents would send a child to school this way, so she visited his house. She found that he lived in a large shack. Her visit revealed that Tommy's mother had died and that his father was working long hours just so the family could survive. There just wasn't enough money to take care of the large family that Tommy lived in. There was no hot water nor electricity in the home. During the teacher's visit to the home, one of Tommy's sisters was washing clothes in a tub filled with cold water. This younger sister didn't even have soap to clean the clothes.

At school Tommy had no friends. He worked hard at showing the other children that it didn't matter to him whether he had friends or not. Some days he would stand on his desk and tell the children in his class that he hated them. He refused to go outside for recess or lunch because that was when the other children were the most cruel to him.

The teacher wanted Tommy and the other children to get along. She tried everything she could think of to get them to accept each other, but nothing seemed to work. As she tried to think of a solution, she thought of William. William was one of her best students and the rest of the class respected him. The thing she admired the most was his kind and considerate nature. She believed that if she could somehow get Tommy and William to be friends, the rest of the class would accept Tommy.

She talked to William privately and explained to him how much Tommy needed to have a friend. She asked him if he would be willing to try to be friends with Tommy, even if Tommy didn't want to be friends. William said he would give it a try.

When the next recess began, William went up to Tommy and asked him to go out and play with him. Tommy said he didn't want to play with him and slugged William right in the nose, knocking him to the floor. Most of us would have jumped up and hit him back, but William got up and said, "I don't care what you do to me; I'm going to be your friend." Tommy yelled at him and said he didn't want a friend, and he knocked William to the floor again. When William got up the second time with the same response as before, Tommy again knocked him to the floor. But William was not going to quit. When he got up this time, Tommy didn't hit him. Now he realized that William meant what he said, and that William loved him no matter what Tommy did.

William's unconditional love changed Tommy. He still had some problems and learning disabilities, but when the other children saw that William had become friends with him they too began to like him. Because he now felt loved, Tommy began to get along better with the others—and, most important, with himself. (See Burgess and Molgard, *Stories That Teach Gospel Principles* [Salt Lake City: Bookcraft, 1989], pp. 5–6.)

The choice to love unconditionally or to hate is ours to make. "And the Messiah cometh in the fulness of time, that he may redeem the children of men from the fall. And because that they are redeemed from the fall they have become free forever, knowing good from evil; to act for themselves and not to be acted upon." (2 Nephi 2:26.)

While Linda was growing up, her mother was an alcoholic. She had a great deal of love for her mother but her mother's drinking caused Linda great embarrassment. All the residents in the little Utah community knew that Linda's mother was an alcoholic. Night after night her parents fought, usually over her mother's drinking problem.

Linda wanted so much to have a mother like her friends had. She wanted to be able to be proud of her mother. Even though her mother was good to her and loved her, it was hard for Linda to enjoy this love because the drinking and fighting got in the way.

By the time Linda reached seventh grade it seemed to her that her mother was never sober. Linda's father tried everything he knew to save the marriage, but he could no longer live with the situation. At last, however, Linda's mother left the family, and she never returned.

Linda was left with many bitter and hurt feelings. As she grew to womanhood she made a commitment to herself that she would be the kind of mother to her children that her mother never was to her. Today Linda has a beautiful family and is a wonderful mother.

Linda found that as she focused her energy toward preparing to be a good mother and eventually made that commitment a reality, she had no time for bitterness and hatred toward her mother. Instead, she found herself loving her mother unconditionally, which brought the peace that only the Spirit could provide.

As we act out our lives and fill them with thoughts and actions of love, bad circumstances can be changed to good. Unconditional love is one of the hardest things we may be called upon to give. We may do everything in our power to love yet still find ourselves falling short of the mark. It is at this point that we must rely on the grace of God to fill the gap. We are forced to reach to a higher power for the help we need. As we reach to that higher source, through the Spirit our Father in Heaven will provide the strength, courage, and power that are necessary to love others unconditionally.

King Benjamin taught:

> The natural man is an enemy to God, and has been from the fall of Adam, and will be, forever and ever, unless he yields to the enticings of the Holy Spirit, and putteth off the natural man and becometh a saint through the atonement of Christ the Lord, and becometh as a child, submissive, meek, humble, patient, full of love, willing to submit to all things which the Lord seeth fit to inflict upon him, even as a child doth submit to his father (Mosiah 3:19).

We could say that the natural man is an enemy to love and that love can change the natural man. I was once in a store pushing my cart down the aisle, minding my own business, when a lady behind me jammed her cart into the back of my heel, ripping my shoe off. My first reaction was that of the natural man. I wanted to turn around and jam her cart into her stomach while asking her why she wasn't paying attention. Before I could do either, she totally disarmed me. She began to apologize for accidentally hitting me and asked me to forgive her. The Spirit quickly took over, and I found myself saying it was all right, even though the natural man said it wasn't. Love will eventually win out over the natural man. The natural man chases the Spirit away, while love invites the Spirit by repelling the natural man.

Jesus' first miracle recorded in the New Testament was that of changing water to wine. If Jesus can change common water into wine, through the Spirit he surely can change common man into something great and marvelous.

The following are some suggestions for improving our invitation to the Spirit through love.

1. *Learn to love yourself.* Remember God's counsel to "love thy neighbour as thyself" (Leviticus 19:18). We must learn to love ourselves before we can give genuine love to others. Our love for ourselves should be unconditional. We don't need a list of reasons verifying our worth. We are important on the sole basis that we are children of God. God has told us the worth of a soul is great in his sight; the whisperings of worthlessness come from Satan.

2. *Be willing to take the first step.* Love can break the bands of hatred. As we express love, through either action or deed, the Spirit will perform miracles in breaking down fences that have stood for years. Pride usually stops us from taking the first step. We must first humble ourselves and call upon God, asking for the courage and wisdom to take the first loving step.

3. *Ask yourself often whether your love is conditional or unconditional.* Don't always look for a return on your investment when you give love. Try offering love with no strings attached. Remember Jesus' teachings: "But I say unto you, Love your enemies, bless them that curse you, do good to them that hate you, and pray for them which despitefully use you, and persecute you; that ye may be the children of your

Father which is in heaven: for he maketh his sun to rise on the evil and on the good, and sendeth rain on the just and on the unjust. For if ye love them which love you, what reward have ye? do not even the publicans the same?" (Matthew 5:45–46.)

4. *Look for those who truly need your love.* Usually, those you find will be those who need unconditional love. Remember that "the person who has earned love the least needs it the most" (F. Enzio Busche, *Ensign,* May 1982, p. 70). "And Jesus answering said unto them, They that are whole need not a physician; but they that are sick" (Luke 5:31).

5. *Ask forgiveness of and express love to someone with whom you have had a disagreement.* "Wherefore, I say unto you, that ye ought to forgive one another; for he that forgiveth not his brother his trespasses standeth condemned before the Lord; for there remaineth in him the greater sin. I, the Lord, will forgive whom I will forgive, but of you it is required to forgive all men." (D&C 64:9–10.)

6. *Maintain and make deposits in a love bank account.* In all of your relationships never make a withdrawal from your love bank account unless you have made deposits to cover the withdrawal. Use this rule: For every withdrawal make ten deposits. All of us have times when circumstances strain our relationships with others. If we have won a person's heart with love, we will have that love to draw on to pull us through the difficult times.

7. *Express love, in both word and deed, every day to those around you.* "Love is the essence of the gospel and the guiding light for a Christlike life. It not only teaches us to look upward but also to look around us." (Hans B. Ringger, *Ensign,* May 1990, p. 26.)

3

An Invitation Through Service

John and Doris Owens had joined the Church in Ireland and had moved to Brigham City, Utah, with their children. The people of Brigham City immediately fell in love with the Owens family. Their love for people and their Irish accents quickly won them a special spot not only in their ward but also throughout the community.

Several years later, John was diagnosed with cancer. As the months wore on he became weaker and more ill. His only regret was that he would not again be able to see the family members he had left in Ireland.

The family was overwhelmed with the financial strain caused by John's sickness. They had no money beyond the payment of the medical bills. One day the family's television stopped working.

A television is important for someone so ill. John had worked at Thiokol Chemical Corporation, and the members of his former carpool now decided to gather money to buy him a new color television. The wives of the men, knowing that others would want to be involved in helping the Owens family, began making some calls. The idea and the money mushroomed.

Soon the Owenses were presented with two tickets to Ireland. They were also given money to spend while they were there. They went to Ireland, visited the relatives, and had a wonderful three weeks.

John passed away two weeks after they returned to Brigham City. Doris still had some of the money that their friends had collected, and when she asked what she should do with the remaining money her friends told her it was hers. They suggested that she stock her shelves with food, but she didn't take that suggestion. Instead she put it away and watched for someone else in need.

Several months later the daughter of a family in the ward became ill with a kidney disease. She would not be well without a kidney transplant. She lived in a city in the East, and her parents longed to be with her but didn't have the money to get there. Doris gladly passed her remaining money on to that family.

She said that she was given so much at the time she and John needed help, and that she would spend the rest of her life looking for ways to help others. Doris felt it was the only way to repay those who had helped her. And she continued to pass it on.

There is no doubt that in the Owens situation the Spirit came readily and was felt by both John and Doris as well as by those who provided this great act of service. Whenever we offer service to others, both those giving and those receiving will benefit by having the Spirit present. As Barbara Winder said, "Peace can come to both the giver and the receiver as we follow the promptings of the Spirit to serve one another" (*Ensign,* November 1985, p. 96).

Those who render true service will feel the Spirit and have their lives transformed. Elder Derek A. Cuthbert explained it as follows: "Service changes people. It refines, purifies, gives a finer perspective, and brings out the best in each one of us. It gets us looking outward instead of inward. It prompts us to consider others' needs ahead of our own. Righteous service is the expression of true charity, such as the Savior showed." (Conference Report, April 1990, p. 12, hereafter cited as CR.)

On the other hand, selfishness, the opposite of service, will drive the Spirit away. "Of all influences that cause men to choose wrong, selfishness is undoubtedly the strongest. Where it is, the Spirit is not." (William R. Bradford, *Ensign,* November 1987, p. 76.)

President Heber J. Grant explained the contrast between service and selfishness in this way: "There are two spirits striving with all men—one telling them what to do that is right, and one telling them what to do that will please themselves, that will gratify their own pride and ambition." (CR, April 1938, p. 12.)

The Spirit of the Lord will always inspire us to serve. The spirit of Satan will prompt us to think of self before others. Satan's influence will drive from us the desire to serve, in which case service will be replaced by self-gratification and sin. If we are going to truly invite the Spirit into our lives, we must first overcome our selfish desires.

Elder Richard G. Scott has taught: "Where selfishness and transgression flourish, the Spirit of the Lord can't enter your life to bless you. To succeed, you must conquer your selfishness. When your beacon is focused on self, it does little more than blind your vision.

When turned outward through acts of kindness and love, it will light your path to happiness and peace." (*Ensign,* May 1990, p. 74.)

We must be careful that we understand the difference between the kind of service the Lord teaches and the false service that Satan teaches. The service Satan teaches disguises selfishness under the cloak of service. Some serve with strings attached, or because it is personally advantageous. Some are offended if their service is not appreciated. Others only serve those who they feel are worthy of such service or do it only out of obligation. Regardless of the service rendered, if the service is based on selfish motives the Spirit will not attend such service. Regarding this kind of service, President Spencer W. Kimball stated: "You are missing all the dessert. You are getting only the hard potatoes." (Edward L. Kimball, ed., *The Teachings of Spencer W. Kimball* [Salt Lake City: Bookcraft, 1982], p. 480, hereafter cited as *SWK Teachings.*)

In contrast, service given unconditionally will bring the Spirit into the lives of those giving and those receiving.

> A selfless person is one who is more concerned about the happiness and well-being of another than about his or her own convenience or comfort, one who is willing to serve another when it is neither sought for nor appreciated, or one who is willing to serve even those whom he or she dislikes. A selfless person displays a willingness to sacrifice, a willingness to purge from his or her mind and heart personal wants, and needs, and feelings. Instead of reaching for and requiring praise and recognition for himself, or gratification of his or her own wants, the selfless person will meet these very human needs for others. (H. Burke Peterson, *Ensign,* May 1985, p. 66.)

The following are some suggestions for improving our relationship with the Spirit through service.

1. *Small and simple things truly matter.* Some of the greatest acts ever performed are the simple and small ones. It is the little daily acts of service that make the difference in people's lives. The Lord counseled: "Wherefore, be not weary in well-doing, for ye are laying the foundation of a great work. And out of small things proceedeth that which is great." (D&C 64:33.)

President Spencer W. Kimball taught:

> God does notice us, and he watches over us. But it is usually through another mortal that he meets our needs. Therefore, it is vital that we serve each other in the kingdom. . . .
>
> So often, our acts of service consist of simple encouragement or of giving mundane help with mundane tasks—but what glorious consequences can flow from mundane acts and from small but deliberate deeds! (*SWK Teachings*, p. 252.)

2. *Personal problems can be solved through service to others.* As we struggle with problems in our own lives, they can be solved through the influence of the Spirit as we serve others. President Ezra Taft Benson has taught:

> To lose yourself in righteous service to others can lift your sights and get your mind off personal problems, or at least put them in proper focus. "When you find yourselves a little gloomy," said President Lorenzo Snow, "look around you and find somebody that is in a worse plight than yourself; go to him and find out what the trouble is, then try to remove it with the wisdom which the Lord bestows upon you; and the first thing you know, your gloom is gone, you feel light, the Spirit

of the Lord is upon you, and everything seems illuminated. (CR, 6 April 1899, pp. 2–3.)" (CR, October 1974, p. 91.)

President Spencer W. Kimball taught that it is by serving that we learn how to serve. When we serve others, not only do they benefit but also we see our problems more clearly. President Kimball said: "In the midst of the miracle of serving, there is the promise of Jesus, that by losing ourselves, we find ourselves. Not only do we 'find' ourselves in terms of acknowledging guidance in our lives, but the more we serve our fellowmen in appropriate ways, the more substance there is to our souls." (*SWK Teachings*, p. 254.)

Elder Russell M. Nelson commented on the attitude his father displayed after losing his wife: "When someone asked how he was doing, my father simply stated, 'I'm lonely, but I'm not lonesome.' Do you know what he meant? Though he was now without his sweetheart, he was so busy assisting family and friends, he had replaced sorrow with service and had displaced self-pity with selfless love. He had found joy in following the timeless example of the Master." (*Ensign*, November 1985, p. 32.)

3. *The greater the effort and sacrifice, the greater the outpouring of the Spirit.* Unconditional service sometimes requires great personal sacrifice and effort. Many times the Lord asks us to serve when it is not convenient or easy. If we obey when he does this he also pours out his Spirit to aid and bless us. Elder Spencer W. Kimball taught:

> I find that sometimes when I have skimped on my time and my efforts, I feel a loss of the intensity of the Spirit.
>
> But, when I do not limit my time or efforts, and

lose myself in . . . [others'] needs, I find myself somewhat in the position mentioned by the Prophet Joseph, who said, ". . . Great things shall be accomplished by you from this hour; and you shall begin to feel the whisperings of the Spirit of God; and the work of God shall begin to break forth from this time; and you shall be endowed with power from on high." (*History of the Church* 2:182.) (*SWK Teachings,* p. 177.)

4. *Learn to serve anonymously.* Look for regular opportunities to serve anonymously. One of the best ways to test our motives for offering service is to do it anonymously. Only you and the Lord should know that you are doing it, as in the case of the Lord's instructions on giving alms:

> Take heed that ye do not your alms before men, to be seen of them: otherwise ye have no reward of your Father which is in heaven.
>
> Therefore when thou doest thine alms, do not sound a trumpet before thee, as the hypocrites do in the synagogues and in the streets, that they may have glory of men. Verily I say unto you, They have their reward.
>
> But when thou doest alms, let not thy left hand know what thy right hand doeth:
>
> That thine alms may be in secret: and thy Father which seeth in secret himself shall reward thee openly. (Matthew 6:1–4.)

When I think of this statement, I feel sure that the Lord gives us blessings we are not even conscious of, as well as obvious ones. In a sense, we could say he gives us these blessings anonymously. Therefore we should thank him on a regular basis for the things he does for us of which we may not be aware.

Elder David B. Haight described the benefits of this kind of service when he stated: "Those who labor unselfishly in behalf of others, with no thought of remuneration, will be physically and spiritually refreshed and renewed" (*Ensign,* May 1990, p. 25).

5. *Be willing to receive.* Often it is easier to serve than it is to receive help from someone. All of us need to learn to accept acts of service from others. When we graciously receive these acts of service we are also being of service to those who are serving us. By letting others do things for us we are building a bond of friendship and love.

The following story is a good example of this principle.

Bishop Hansen had spent a great deal of time encouraging the ward members to look for ways to fellowship new and less-active members of the ward. He felt a great responsibility to follow his own counsel.

When Kyle and his family moved in across the street, the bishop went straight over and introduced himself. His welcome was not received in a friendly manner. It appeared that Kyle was not interested in the Church or in being a friend of Bishop Hansen's. Bishop Hansen regularly offered to help him but Kyle refused his help. This was very frustrating to the bishop.

As time passed he pondered on how he could gain Kyle's friendship. To that point in time none of his attempts had been successful. One day he tried something new. He had a cattle rack on the back of his pickup. He and his son removed the rack from the truck. Then he went over to Kyle's and asked if Kyle could help him put the rack on his truck. Kyle said he would be glad to. From that point on, Kyle and Bishop Hansen's friendship increased. After Kyle had helped him several times in this way, Kyle began accepting and even asking for help from the bishop.

6. *Remember, there is no greater investment.* Steve and Debbie owned a car that was well worn, since they had purchased it from a used car dealer ten years before. It now had over a hundred thousand miles on it, the seats were threadbare, the paint was faded, and there was always something wrong with it. Each time it went into the shop, Steve would tell Debbie that the time had come for them to buy a new car. In the past they had just done without the luxury of a new car because most of their money had been spent in rearing their four children. But now, with their children older, they were in a position to save enough money to make a substantial down payment on a new car. In all of their married life they had never been able to afford a new car; now, it looked as though the long-awaited day had come.

They went down to the car dealership and picked out the new car they wanted, but decided to wait until the next day to purchase the car. As they drove home, excitement about the prospects of buying their first new car could be felt in the air.

That evening as thoughts about purchasing the new car ran through their minds they started to have some misgivings. Was their family really complete? The more they talked, the more they felt that someone was missing. As they discussed the possibilities of having another child, they realized they had an important decision to make. Putting the car purchase on hold, they eventually decided to have another baby.

They did have another child—a little girl. The money they had saved for the new car was used on hospital and doctor expenses.

Now it is eighteen years later. Steve and Debbie are driving home from a high school graduation. Sitting in the front seat of the car in between them is a beautiful daughter who has just graduated from high school. As they drive along, Steve's and Debbie's hearts are full of pride and joy, for over the years this wonderful daughter has brought them indescribable happiness. As they round the curve in the highway Steve and Debbie see something that catches their attention—a junkyard full of cars. Scanning the pile of smashed cars, they see on the top of the stack a burned-out, rusted hull of the exact model of car they had wanted to buy eighteen years before. Looking at their daughter and then back at the car, Steve and Debbie clasp hands and smile secretly to each other.

They had been greatly blessed for their decision, and feelings of love for their daughter filled their souls that evening.

As this couple so dramatically learned, there is only one thing that will last forever: the investment we make in the lives of other people. The things of this world will rust and waste away but the children of God are eternal. The time spent serving mankind will bring not only immediate blessings of the Spirit but also eternal joy in the world to come.

This principle is reflected in the Lord's words:

> Remember the worth of souls is great in the sight of God. . . . And if it so be that you should labor all your days in crying repentance unto this people, and bring, save it be one soul unto me, how great shall be your joy with him in the kingdom of my Father!
>
> And now, if your joy will be great with one soul that you have brought unto me into the kingdom of my Father, how great will be your joy if you should bring many souls unto me! (D&C 18:10, 15–16.)

4

An Invitation Through Prayer

Rebecca was on her way to the Nixons' to babysit. As she walked down the sidewalk, her mind drifted back to her first babysitting job several months before. She remembered how nervous she had been and how keenly she had wanted to do a good job. Since that first job she had tended many of the neighborhood children several times. She was no longer nervous and her confidence grew with each experience.

As she arrived at the Nixons' door the children, Janice and Doug, were looking out of the front bay window. Before Rebecca could even knock they quickly opened the door, then hugged her as she walked into the front room. They loved her and were excited to have her as their babysitter that evening. She had never babysat for the Nixons, but had sat beside them in church and had watched the children from the time they had been born. Janice and Doug had begged their parents to ask Rebecca to babysit.

Brother and Sister Nixon were going out to dinner and then to a play—they wouldn't be home until after midnight. As they were leaving they gave Rebecca some last-minute instructions: the children were to be in bed by ten o'clock and she could go to sleep on the couch if she got tired. This was a relief to Rebecca, because she hated fighting to stay awake until the parents got home.

The evening went by quickly. Rebecca and the kids watched two of their favorite shows on television and then played a couple of the children's games. By that time it was nine-forty-five—time for Janice and Doug to go to bed. They were tired and went right to bed.

Rebecca sighed as she walked down the stairs. She felt so tired. After checking the locks on the front door and the sliding door off the dining room, she turned on the porch light. She took the afghan off the back of the couch, lay down, and went to sleep.

Rebecca was awakened suddenly by a rattle at the sliding door in the dining room. She knew she had locked all of the doors before lying down. Who could this be? Her heart raced as she looked at the clock on the wall; it read eleven-fifteen. This couldn't be the Nixons—it was too early.

She jumped up and peeked carefully around the corner to see if she could tell who or what was making the noise. Her heart beat even more wildly when she saw a figure of a man at the door.

She ran down the hall to Brother and Sister Nixon's bedroom. As she entered that room she breathed a sigh of relief; there was a phone by the side of their bed. She quickly picked up the phone and dialed 911. One ring, and a voice responded, "911, how can I help you?"

Rebecca explained in a quiet, panic-stricken voice, "There is a man trying to break into the house!" The voice on the other end asked, "Where are you?" Rebecca heard a loud crash of glass breaking in the dining room. In a low but terrified voice she spoke into the phone, "He's broken the sliding door! Help me . . . Please help me!" The person on the other end of the phone responded, "Help is on the way." With that Rebecca hung up the phone and hid herself underneath the bed.

Immediately, a terrifying thought entered her mind: in her panic, she hadn't given 911 a name or an address. But she was too frightened to come out from beneath the bed. With tears running down her cheeks, she waited.

After what seemed like an eternity (but in reality was only a few minutes) Rebecca could hear a great deal of commotion in the kitchen. Her heart increased its pounding and she backed closer to the wall as she saw two feet come into the bedroom. Then she heard a voice say, "Don't be frightened. I'm a policeman. Everything is all right."

Rebecca moved slowly and carefully as she peeked out from under the bed. She relaxed as she saw an officer in full uniform. "But how did you know where I was? I forgot to tell the person who answered the phone."

The officer smiled and explained that as soon as a person calls 911, the phone number, address, and name of the phone owner appear on the computer screen. This marvelous system had saved Rebecca and the children from the intruder.

If man, with his limited mind, can establish a system as marvelous as the 911 system, is it stretching the imagination to accept that God can hear and answer all of his children's prayers? It also should be no wonder that God knows each of us by name and understands our individual needs. He is always there, just like the operators of the 911 system. And just as with the 911 system, we must initiate the call to make the connection. As soon as we make the call, Heavenly Father knows who it is that is calling and where we are. Like the operators, he is willing to help us. As we express to him our needs and concerns he can activate powers and forces in our behalf.

One of the major ways he assists us is through the Holy Ghost. It is through this medium that he reveals his will and imparts to us comfort and peace.

A prayer of faith can quickly bring the Spirit to us in times of need. Satan understands this principle very well. We need to realize that it is Satan's influence and spirit that prompts us not to pray. In the Book of Mormon, Nephi taught:

> If ye would hearken unto the Spirit which teacheth a man to pray ye would know that ye must pray; for the evil spirit teacheth not a man to pray, but teacheth him that he must not pray. But behold, I say unto you that ye must pray always, and not faint; that ye must not perform any thing unto the Lord save in the first place ye shall pray unto the Father in the name of Christ, that he will consecrate thy performance unto thee, that thy performance may be for the welfare of thy soul. (2 Nephi 32:8–9.)

We learn from Nephi that the time we don't feel like praying is the time when we need to pray the most. Satan doesn't want us to pray, because he knows too well that prayer is one of the most effective ways of inviting the Spirit into our lives.

Brigham Young taught:

If you find [anger] coming on you, go off to some place where you cannot be heard; let none of your family see you or hear you; and pray for strength to overcome. . . . And if, when the time for prayer comes, you have not the spirit of prayer upon you, and your knees are unwilling to bow, say to them, "Knees, get down there;" make them bend, and remain there until you obtain the Spirit of the Lord. (*Journal of Discourses,* 11:290.)

Often when something important is about to take place in a person's life, Satan will try to stop it. The prophets have learned this lesson well. Before Adam and Eve began their great mortal existence, Satan came tempting them. On one occasion, before Moses saw and spoke with God face to face, Satan appeared in all his power. Before Joseph Smith saw the Father and the Son, Satan came upon him and tried to destroy him. In each of these incidents the prophet prayed to the Father, was delivered from Satan's influence, and then received a glorious manifestation from God.

So it is with each one of us. As we are about to make spiritual progress in our lives, the father of lies will be there to try to stop it from happening. We need to know, however, that just because we feel the influence of Satan in our lives at some point does not mean we are evil. Frequently Satan's temptations and influences come upon us because we are making righteous progress and he wants to stop that process. President Kimball taught: "We are all very much aware, my brothers and sisters, that the world is in turmoil. We are continually being tried and tested as individuals and as a church. There are more trials yet to come, but be not discouraged nor dismayed. Always remember that if this were not the Lord's work, the adversary would not pay any attention to us." (*Ensign,* May 1981, p. 79.)

Prayer is one of the most powerful ways of overcoming the influence of Satan. The Lord instructed us: "Pray always, that you may come off conqueror; yea, that you may conquer Satan, and that you may escape the hands of the servants of Satan that do uphold his work" (D&C 10:5). When a depressive influence comes upon us we need to remember to turn to the one source that can deliver us. The Savior taught his disciples that "this kind can come forth by nothing, but by prayer and fasting" (Mark 9:29).

As we have faith in Heavenly Father and his power and turn to him in prayer, the Spirit can quickly lift us to higher ground. "Prayer in the hour of need is a great boon. From simple trials to our Gethsemanes, prayer can put us in touch with God, our greatest source of comfort and counsel." (Ezra Taft Benson, CR, October 1974, p. 91.)

The following are some suggestions that can help us as we use prayer to invite the Spirit into our lives.

1. *Pray anytime, anywhere, anyhow.* "A mammoth 747 jetliner, while flying over the Pacific, sustained a gigantic tear in its side, ejecting nine passengers to their deaths, and threatening the lives of all. When the pilot, Captain David Cronin, was interviewed, having brought the craft back safely to Honolulu, he was asked, 'What did you do when the plane ripped open? How did you cope?'

"Captain Cronin replied, 'I prayed, then went to work.'

"My brethren, this is an inspired plan for each of us to follow: Pray, and then go to work." (Thomas S. Monson, *Ensign,* May 1989, p. 44.)

During the day and week there are times when we should have formal prayers. For example, at the beginning and ending of meetings, as blessings on the food, family prayer, and personal prayer morning and night.

But we must also remember that, as long as we are reverent in attitude, we can pray anytime, anywhere, and virtually anyhow—that is, either verbally or mentally, and in any position or circumstances as the need arises. It is hard to imagine that Captain Cronin let go of the controls, knelt on the floor of the plane, and closed his eyes while he offered his prayer. Some of the most sincere prayers ever offered are uttered with our eyes wide open, while we are in the middle of something, and even without spoken words.

In the case of many of the prayers we offer "anytime, anywhere, and anyhow," we don't really finish praying. The prayer just stays in our hearts until it is answered; then our prayer changes and we offer a prayer of gratitude.

There is never a bad time to pray. We must never forget that Heavenly Father and Jesus are available anytime we need them. We may forget them, but they will never forget us. "But, behold, Zion hath said: The Lord hath forsaken me, and my Lord hath forgotten me—but he will show that he hath not. For can a woman forget her sucking child, that she should not have compassion on the son of her womb? Yea, they may forget, yet will I not forget thee, O house of Israel. Behold, I have graven thee upon the palms of my hands; thy walls are continually before me." (1 Nephi 21:14–16.)

2. *Wait before, during, and after your prayers.* The phone rings. You pick it up and hear this on the other end: "Hi, John, how are you? I just called to say hi. Could you please send me some money and could you please help me with my homework? And I'm leaving to go on vacation; could you feed my dog? By the way, you've been to California. Where is the best place to get discount tickets for Disneyland? Well, I've got to run; have a nice day. Good-bye. [Click.]"

If all of our incoming phone calls were like this one, there would be no need for us to have a mouthpiece on our phone. But in fact our prayers frequently are too much like it. We pray to Heavenly Father, asking, telling, and expressing, but we never take time to listen to what he has to say. By waiting before, during, and after, we can give him time to talk, and we can listen.

President Spencer W. Kimball taught us:

> Is prayer only one-way communication? No! . . . At the end of our prayers, we need to do some intense listening—even for several minutes. We have prayed for counsel and help. . . .
>
> Sometimes ideas flood our mind as we listen after our prayers. Sometimes feelings press upon us. A spirit of calmness assures us that all will be well. But always, if we have been honest and earnest, we will experience a good feeling—a feeling of warmth for our Father in Heaven and a sense of his love for us. (*Ensign,* October 1981, p. 5.)

As you kneel in prayer, wait a few moments before praying. As you wait, ponder on who it is you are about to pray to. Think about the things you want to pray about and who needs your prayers. Focus your mind and heart before beginning your prayer.

Once you have started your prayer, don't be afraid to stop during the prayer and listen. Give Heavenly Father a chance to respond to your questions, concerns, and requests.

After you have formally closed your prayer, stay on your knees for a little while and again give Heavenly Father a chance to speak to your mind and heart.

3. *Pray for others.* Amulek taught: "let your hearts

be full, drawn out in prayer unto him continually for your welfare, and also for the welfare of those who are around you" (Alma 34:27). The Spirit will quickly fill our souls when we pray for those around us and even for those we might not know or those who may have offended us. Enos's experience was a good example of this. He first prayed for his own soul and then for the welfare of his brethren, the Nephites. Then he prayed "with many long strugglings" for the Lamanites. As he did this, he had many rewarding experiences with the Spirit. This can be our experience also. Each time we offer a prayer to Heavenly Father we should consider those who need our prayers and bring their names before him. We should also ask for guidance where possible and pray for revelation on how we can be of service to those we are praying for.

As we pray for those we may not get along with, we need to make sure our motives are righteous. A good question we might ask is, "Am I praying for them so they won't bother me, or am I really praying for their welfare?" As we do this, not only will our lives be filled with the Spirit but also the lives of those we pray for will be blessed.

4. *Pray to be forgiven.* In the New Testament we read that the future parents of John the Baptist, Zacharias and Elisabeth, "were both righteous before God, walking in all the commandments and ordinances of the Lord blameless" (Luke 1:6). Elisabeth had been barren and apparently was now past the normal age to have children. It seems likely that they both had spent a great deal of time over the years praying to the Lord about having a child. Yet no answer came until after many years had passed. When the angel Gabriel appeared to Zacharias he announced, "Thy prayer is heard; and thy wife Elisabeth shall bear thee a son, and thou shalt call his name John" (Luke 1:13).

We might ask the question, "Why was their prayer an-swered?" The answer to that question can be found in a statement in verse 6—their prayer was answered be-cause they were blameless before the Lord.

The best way to have clear and open communica-tion with Heavenly Father is to be clean before him. One of the things that can bring the Spirit to us as we pray is to first recognize our sins and confess them to God in prayer. As we honestly ask for his forgiveness he will bless us with his Spirit.

5

An Invitation Through the Sacrament

Scott kissed Janet good-bye and went out of the front door. As soon as he stepped onto the front porch, he knew this day was going to begin as so many had before. He could see garbage strewn all over the carport and underneath Janet's car. With his blood pressure rising, he slammed the front door and ran towards the mess.

"That rotten dog," he muttered to himself. "This really makes me mad!" The more garbage he picked up, the angrier he became.

It would be different if this was the first time, or even the first time this week; but it felt like an overused rerun. The eggshells were so hard to pick up that they especially irritated him. By the time he had all of the garbage picked up, his hands were dirty and some gunk from one of the cans had spilled on his pants.

He returned to the house to wash his hands and change his suit. (That suit had just been cleaned, and now it was on its way to the cleaner again.)

Janet came into the bedroom to see why Scott was back in the house. Before she could say anything, he unloaded on her. "I'm going to kill that dog!" he shouted.

"The garbage again?" Janet asked.

"Yes, and this is the last straw," Scott yelled. "As soon as I get home from work, if I ever get to work, I'm going to talk to George about it!" With that, he stomped out of the house.

Scott spent the rest of the day rehearsing what he was going to say to George. He couldn't understand why George just let his dog run loose during the night. Scott knew it was George's dog that was getting into the garbage, because he had seen it doing so on several occasions. In fact, a couple of times he had pulled into the driveway late at night, only to see the dog running from the carport.

As Scott arrived home that evening he noticed George's car parked on the street. Rather than put it off, he decided he might as well go right over and talk to George. George and Scott had been neighbors for twenty-three years and had never had any problems. That is, no problems until now.

As George came to the door, twenty-three years of being a good neighbor began to unravel. Scott had gotten himself so worked up thinking about the dog all day that not one word he said to George came out right. To make things worse, George was not the type of person who liked people telling him what to do, and that was exactly what Scott was doing. He was telling George that unless he kept his dog locked up, Scott was going to kill it. Needless to say, the conversation went nowhere fast. George slammed his door and Scott stomped across the street mumbling something about George being a pig-headed fool.

Several days went by with no further trouble. Scott was even starting to feel a little remorseful about how he had acted with George. He knew he had approached the whole matter the wrong way. He knew that if he had stated his concern in the right way, George would have responded favorably.

It was Sunday morning, and as Scott and his family went to get into the car to go to church there it was—garbage everywhere! Scott and his two boys jumped out of the car and began to clean up the mess. The more they cleaned, the more upset Scott became. All of the remorse he had felt about how he had talked to George left him. He told the two boys to get into the car—he would be right back. He went straight over to George's house and banged on the door; and this time he totally lost control. Instead of mumbling, he simply looked George in the face and called him a pig-headed fool. With that, George ordered him off his property, threatening to call the police. Scott made his way back to the car, where his family was waiting. By this time Janet was so embarrassed that she was in tears. This made Scott even more angry, which was evident by the way he maneuvered the car on their way to the church.

They all went in and sat in their usual place (third row back, center section, right side). Scott just sat there and stewed. It had been a long time since he was this mad; he was totally consumed with anger. As he sat fuming, he looked over at the priests sitting at the sacrament table. At that moment he knew he needed to resolve the problem between him and George before he could feel comfortable in taking the sacrament. He turned around to see if George and his family had arrived, and at that moment they just happened to be coming through the door. Scott left his seat, went back, and asked George if he could talk to him in the foyer. There in the foyer Scott apologized for his behavior and asked George to forgive him. It was a short conversation—George said he would try to forgive Scott, and then they hurried back into the chapel before the meeting began.

Scott knew that his words of apology were only a beginning to making things right with George. All he could think about during the announcements and the opening song and prayer was how he could show George that his apology was sincere. He found himself wondering whether he had the strength to love George as he really needed to. Some of the anger still lingered in his heart, even though he had apologized.

But during the sacrament song Scott started to feel a peace coming over him. As he heard the priest start the prayer on the sacrament, he knew he would receive the wisdom and strength he needed. In a very short while one of the deacons was standing at the end of his row with the broken bread, and as the tray was slowly passed down his row, Scott's thoughts raced through all he knew and understood about the sacrament. A feeling of remorse overcame him as he asked Heavenly Father to forgive him for the way he had dealt with George. He then promised Heavenly Father that he would follow through with his commitment to make things right with George.

At this, Scott found the feelings of anger replaced with a peace that only the Spirit can bring. He then took a piece of bread from the sacrament tray and ate it, with a firm resolve to follow through in making things right with George. As he did so, he felt an outpouring of the Spirit, which gave him the hope and determination he needed.

As we attend Church meetings and partake of the

sacrament, the Spirit can come quickly to us as it did to Scott. Not only did it turn his anger to love and peace, but also it helped him make a resolve to change and be better. "As we worthily partake of the sacrament," Elder John H. Groberg observed, "we will sense those things we need to improve in and receive the help and determination to do so. No matter what our problems, the sacrament always gives hope." (*Ensign*, May 1989, p. 38.)

The sacrament serves as food for the spirit. Scott entered the sacrament meeting with a great spiritual hunger and was fed.

Elder Melvin J. Ballard taught:

> How can we have spiritual hunger? Who is there among us that does not wound his spirit by word, thought, or deed, from Sabbath to Sabbath? We do things for which we are sorry and desire to be forgiven, or we have erred against someone and given injury. If there is a feeling in our hearts that we are sorry for what we have done; if there is a feeling in our souls that we would like to be forgiven, then the method to obtain forgiveness is not through rebaptism . . . but it is to repent of our sins, to go to those against whom we have sinned or transgressed and obtain their forgiveness, and then repair to the sacrament table, where, if we have sincerely repented and put ourselves in proper condition, we shall be forgiven, and spiritual healing will come to our souls. (*Improvement Era*, October 1919, p. 1026.)

There is a power that comes with worthily partaking of the sacrament, a power that is not fully understood by mankind. However, this we do know: It provides us with the promise of having the Spirit with us.

If attending sacrament meeting and partaking of the sacrament brings the Spirit to our lives, the opposite is also true: not attending and partaking will cause a loss of the Spirit. With regard to this principle, President Joseph Fielding Smith taught:

> No member of the church can fail to make this covenant [the sacrament] and renew it week by week, and retain the Spirit of the Lord. The Sacrament meeting of the Church is the most important meeting which we have, and is sadly neglected by many members. We go to this service, if we understand the purpose of it, not primarily to hear someone speak, important though that may be, but first, and most important, to renew this covenant with our Father in Heaven in the name of Jesus Christ. Those who persist in their absence from this service will eventually lose the Spirit and if they do not repent will eventually find themselves denying the faith. (*Church History and Modern Revelation,* 1:122–23.)

I know a couple whose son was preparing to be married in the temple. When they went to their bishop to get a temple recommend in order to attend the wedding, the mother admitted that she was drinking coffee daily. The bishop said he could not issue her a recommend until she stopped drinking coffee. He challenged her to stop and promised that the Lord would help her. He pointed out to her that she had plenty of time to stop before the wedding.

Instead of stopping the habit, she left the bishop's office saying that she would never come back to church as long as he was the bishop. She kept her promise and missed her son's wedding. As the years passed and several bishops were sustained and released, she never came back to church. Instead, she lost the Spirit and denied the faith.

The sad story does not end there. Her failure to partake of the sacrament and retain the Spirit not only led her from the great blessings she could have had but it also affected most of her children, who have also lost the Spirit and denounced the Church.

We need to come to an understanding of the great power the sacrament can have in our lives. It serves as a protection against the fiery darts of Satan.

Matthew Cowley tells of a young sailor who came into the Cowley home in New Zealand during World War II. A convert to the Church, he had been ordained a priest before leaving the States and was the only member of the Church on his ship. Elder Cowley asked him how it was being the only member aboard the ship.

His reply was: "Well, whenever we stop at a port, the fellows all come around and kid me and say, 'Come on, let's go out and have a good time, get on a binge, get some relaxation.' But I do not go. You know the reason I do not go? You know the reason I can stand up against those invitations and temptation? It is because the captain of the ship on Sundays gives me a little room, and I go into that little room all by myself. I have that little serviceman's copy of the Book of Mormon, so I take a little water and a piece of bread. I open up the Book of Mormon to Moroni, and I get down on my knees. I bless the sacrament, and I pass it to myself.' And he said, 'Then I am safe for another week.' He said, 'Nobody on earth can tempt me.'" (See Leon R. Hartshorn, *Outstanding Stories by General Authorities,* vol. 2 [Salt Lake City: Deseret Book Co., 1971], p. 73.)

The following are some suggestions for improving our invitation to the Spirit through the sacrament.

1. *Read or memorize the sacrament prayer.* While the sacrament is being passed, read or recite the sacrament prayer to yourself, focusing on the three promises we make when we partake of the sacrament. Elder David O. McKay explained those three promises as follows:

> The first: That we are willing to take upon ourselves the name of the Son. In so doing we choose him as our leader and our ideal; and he is the one perfect character in all the world. It is a glorious thing to be a member of the Church of Christ and to be called a Christian in the true sense of the term; and we promise that we should like to be that, that we are willing to do it.
>
> Secondly, that we will always remember him. Not just on Sunday, but on Monday, in our daily acts, in our self-control. When our brother hurts us are we going to try to master our feelings and not retaliate in the same spirit of anger? When a brother treats us with contempt, are we going to try to return kindness? That's the spirit of the Christ and that's what we are promised—that we will do our best to achieve these high standards of Christianity, true Christian principles.
>
> The third: We promise to 'keep the commandments which he has given.' Tithing, fast offerings, the Word of Wisdom, kindness, forgiveness, love. The obligation of a member of the Church of Christ is great, but it is as glorious as it is great, because obedience to these principles gives life eternal. On the other hand, the man who seeks to live by violating the principles is deceived by the adversary and goes the way to death. (CR, October 1929, pp. 10–11, 14.)

As we keep these promises to God, his promise in return is that we will have his Spirit to be with us. God does not lie. If we keep our promises, his Spirit will be with us.

2. *Think about the mission of the Savior.* During the sacrament, review in your mind the mission of the Savior and all that he did for us. "It is said of President Wilford Woodruff that while the sacrament was being passed, his lips could be observed in silent motion as he repeated to himself over and over again, 'I do remember thee, I do remember thee.'" (Marion G. Romney, *Ensign,* October 1976, p. 3.)

Whenever we think of the Savior and his mission we are inviting the Spirit to be with us. The very mention of his name in a sacred manner will help drive the evil one and his influence from us.

3. *Think about the past week and the week to come.* "The solemn moments of thought while the sacrament is being served have great significance. They are moments of self-examination, introspection, self-discernment—a time to reflect and to resolve." (Howard W. Hunter, *Ensign,* May 1977, p. 25.)

As we examine the past week, we need to "check in" with our Father in Heaven on how we did with our commitments of that week. Then we need to make a resolve on the things for the week to come. A silent prayer to Heavenly Father expressing gratitude, repentance, and commitment is very appropriate and helpful during the sacrament.

6

An Invitation Through the Word of God

Before I left to serve a mission, my mother and I made a commitment. She promised to write a letter to me once a week. In return she made me promise that I would also write once a week.

She faithfully kept her part of the promise, but at times I was not as faithful. Occasionally I had to be prompted with a different letter from my mother. It would state: "This will be the last letter you will receive until I hear from you. In addition, no money will be put in your bank account until you write." You can imagine how quickly I would fire off my letter.

You might think that the threat of an empty wallet was my primary concern, but it wasn't. It was the thought that I would not hear from my mother. Her letters were a source of inspiration and comfort to me. I looked forward each week to receiving a letter from her. Hers was the first to be opened and read. I read her letters more than once; in fact, I savored and treasured each word. Those letters were an immediate boost to me.

As I read her letters, I could clearly hear her voice. It was almost as if she were standing beside me as she told me what was happening at home and offered words of encouragement and direction about the important work I was doing.

Think for a moment of the experience I was having—hearing my mother's voice. How could this be? She was over seven hundred miles away.

Think of someone you know well. Now listen in your mind as they talk to you. You can hear the pitch, the volume, the particular way they have of saying each word. They are speaking to you as my mother spoke to me through the letters she sent.

Heavenly Father's and Jesus' voices are also known to us. We lived with them far longer than we have lived with anyone here in mortality. They have sent and continue to send letters to us through the scriptures and the teachings of the living prophets. These words can have an immediate as well as a long-term effect on us. When we read and study the word of God, the Holy Spirit will come upon us and we will feel and recognize the power of God.

The Savior described it in this way: "And I, Jesus Christ, your Lord and your God, have spoken it. These words are not of men nor of man, but of me; wherefore, you shall testify they are of me and not of man; for it is my voice which speaketh them unto you; for they are given by my Spirit unto you, and by my power you can read them one to another; and save it were by my power you could not have them; wherefore, you can testify that you have heard my voice, and know my words." (D&C 18:33–36.)

One of the best ways we can feel and recognize the power of the Spirit is by searching the word of God. The Prophet Joseph Smith taught: "Search the Scriptures—search the revelations which we publish, and ask your Heavenly Father, in the name of His Son Jesus Christ, to manifest the truth unto you, and if you do it with an eye single to His glory, nothing doubting, He will answer you by the power of His Holy Spirit. You will then know for yourselves and not for another. (*History of the Church* 1:282.)

Satan knows that the word of God is powerful, and therefore he does all he can to draw us away from it. He suggests to us that there isn't time in our busy world to study the word of God. He tells us the scriptures are too hard to understand and that studying them won't make a difference in our lives.

Elder Carlos E. Asay pointed this out beautifully when he stated:

> I fear that many of us rush about from day to day taking for granted the holy scriptures. We scramble to honor appointments with physicians, lawyers, and businessmen. Yet we think nothing of postponing interviews with Deity—postponing scripture study. Little wonder we develop anemic souls and lose our direction in living. How much better it would be if we planned and held sacred fifteen or twenty minutes a day for reading the scriptures. Such interviews with Deity would help us recognize his voice and enable us to receive guidance in all of our affairs. (*Ensign,* November 1978, pp. 53–54.)

Satan promotes many other lies and excuses to draw us away from God's holy word. Why does he do this? Because he knows that the word of God can have such an effect on us that Satan will be bound as far as we are concerned, unable to influence us. President Ezra Taft Benson said: "This is an answer to the great challenge of our time. The word of God, as found in the scriptures, in the words of living prophets, and in personal revelation, has the power to fortify the Saints and arm them with the Spirit so they can resist evil, hold fast to the good, and find joy in this life." (*Ensign*, May 1986, p. 80.)

Satan "seeketh that all men might be miserable like unto himself" (2 Nephi 2:27) and does not want us to have the joy the Father offers. He is, therefore, bent on leading us away from God's teachings. He would have us read and believe the false teachings of the world rather than the truth found in the word of God. These false teachings will never, worlds without end, bring the Spirit of the Lord to a person's life. However, in contrast, the consistent reading of holy writ will quickly bring the Spirit into our lives and drive Satan's influence from us.

As Nephi interpreted the vision of the tree of life and the meaning of the iron rod, he taught: "And they said unto me: What meaneth the rod of iron which our father saw, that led to the tree? And I said unto them that it was the word of God; and whoso would hearken unto the word of God, and would hold fast unto it, they would never perish; neither could the temptations and the fiery darts of the adversary overpower them unto blindness, to lead them away to destruction." (1 Nephi 15:23–24.)

Some years ago I decided that I wanted to obtain a private pilot's licence. During my training I moved, and I ended up having three different instructors. A few days before I was to be given my "check ride" to receive my licence, my instructor was reviewing with me certain procedures and maneuvers that I would be required to perform. One of the required maneuvers was to recover from a stall. To do this you have to fly the aircraft in a vertical climb until it loses its ability to stay in the air, or in other words, until it stalls. (There isn't a roller coaster ride in the world that can match the feeling you get when the plane drops out of the sky.)

Thinking that I needed a review, my instructor asked me to do a stall. I panicked. I didn't know how to do a stall, and I admitted this to my instructor. He was quite surprised and said that I should have mastered stalls earlier in my training. We surmised that as I had traded instructors each one had assumed that the other had taught or would teach me how to do stalls. He said he knew I would catch on quickly, and he gave me a few brief instructions. Then we were ready to begin.

I proceeded by putting the plane into a vertical climb. As it climbed, keeping it level was critical. If the plane tilts to one side or the other when it stalls, it will go into a spiral spin. Sure enough, when the plane stalled I had it tilted to the left and it went into a spin. I pulled desperately at the controls, trying to pull it out of the spin; but they would not respond. The more I pulled, the more I panicked as the plane refused to come under my control.

Thank goodness I had an instructor with me. He reached over and pulled back on the power, slowing the plane down enough that the controls took hold. Then he was easily able to pull the plane out of the spin. If he hadn't been there I would have drilled a hole in the ground that day.

After we had pulled out of the spin and I had pushed my stomach down and out of my mouth and wiped three gallons of sweat off of my face, he told me to try another one.

This time I was going to make sure I did not allow

the plane to tilt to the left. But I overcompensated and tilted the plane to the right—with the same results as before. After we pulled out of this second spin I told the instructor I was through for the day. My head and stomach had been pushed to the limit. So had my emotions. I was ready to retire from flying permanently; I wanted no part of it.

Fortunately, time faded my memory, and the next day I went back up and performed the stall recovery procedure perfectly.

It was all a matter of balance. The same is true with our lives. We can easily let our spiritual life get out of balance. One of the great balancing agents is the word of God. When our life goes into a spin, one of the things that can pull us out of the spin is studying the word of God. Elder Spencer W. Kimball understood and taught this principle:

> I find that all I need to do to increase my love for my Maker and the gospel and the Church and my brethren is to read the scriptures. I have spent many hours in the scriptures during the last few days. I prescribe that for people who are in trouble. I cannot see how anyone can read the scriptures and not develop a testimony of their divinity and of the work of the Lord, who is the spokesman in the scriptures.
>
> I find that when I get casual in my relationships with divinity and when it seems that no divine ear is listening and no divine voice is speaking, that I am far, far away. If I immerse myself in the scriptures the distance narrows and the spirituality returns. I find myself loving more intensely those whom I must love with all my heart and mind and strength, and loving them more, I find it easier to abide their counsel. (*SWK Teachings,* p. 135.)

Some of us limit the word of God to the standard works of the Church and forget that the teachings of the living prophets are also scripture to us. Those teachings contain just as much power to invite the Spirit into our lives.

In a revelation given to the Prophet Joseph Smith the Lord revealed: "And whatsoever they shall speak when moved upon by the Holy Ghost shall be scripture, shall be the will of the Lord, shall be the mind of the Lord, shall be the word of the Lord, shall be the voice of the Lord, and the power of God unto salvation" (D&C 68:4).

The teachings of the General Authorities of the Church, as given in general conference and then recorded in the *Ensign,* are the word of God to us. With regard to this, President Henry D. Moyle stated:

> The older I get and the closer the contact I have with the President of the Church, the more I realize that the greatest of all scriptures which we have in the world today is current scripture. What the mouthpiece of God says to His children is scripture. It is intended for all the children of God upon the earth. It is His word and His will and His law made manifest through His ordained and anointed servant to the world. What the President says is scripture, and I love it more than all other. It applies to me today specifically, and to you all. ("Beware of Temptation," BYU Tri-stake Fireside, January 1963, pp. 7–8.)

The following are some suggestions for improving our invitation to the Spirit through studying the word of God:

1. *Study every day.* None of us would think of eating only once or twice or even just three times a week.

We eat every day and several times during the day. The same should be true when feeding our spirit on the words of God. Set aside a time and place each day, even if it is just for a few minutes, so that you can study and feed your spirit. Remember that "the scriptures that are never read will never help us" (L. Tom Perry, *Ensign,* May 1985, p. 23).

Elder Bruce R. McConkie gave a plan that would take us through the standard works in less than eighteen months:

> We have the Bible, the Book of Mormon, the Doctrine and Covenants, and the Pearl of Great Price. There are in these four books a total of 1579 chapters. I think it would not be too much to say that we could with propriety, day in and day out, consistently, read three chapters in one or the other of these works; and if we pursued such a course, we would read all of the Gospels in less than a month. We would read the entire New Testament in ten months, and the whole Bible in thirteen months. We would go through the Book of Mormon in two and two-thirds months, the Doctrine and Covenants in a month and a half, and the Pearl of Great Price in five days. Taken altogether, we would read all the standard works in less than eighteen months and be ready to start over again. (CR, October 1959, p. 51.)

2. *Ponder.* As you study the words of God stop from time to time and ponder on what you have read. Elder Marvin J. Ashton has taught:

> By pondering, we give the Spirit an opportunity to impress and direct. Pondering is a powerful link between the heart and the mind. As we read the

scriptures, our hearts and minds are touched. If we use the gift to ponder, we can take these eternal truths and realize how we can incorporate them into our daily actions. . . .

We find understanding, insight, and practical application if we will use the gift of pondering. (*Ensign,* November 1987, p. 20.)

3. *Use basic skills of scripture study.* Following are some basic skills that can help us benefit more from our study of the scriptures:

A. *Use chapter headings.* Read the chapter headings before reading the chapter. By doing so you gain an overview of what you are about to read.

B. *Identify key words.* As you read, circle or underline words that are a key to the verse you are studying. Stop and ask yourself this question: If I could leave only five words in this verse, and still retain the meaning, what words would they be? By doing this, you will be able to focus on the real message of the passage.

C. *Identify and look up difficult words.* When you run into words you don't understand, look up their meanings in the Bible dictionary or a regular dictionary.

D. *Use the footnotes.* When you are having trouble in understanding a passage, check the footnotes for further help.

E. *Make personal application.* Follow Nephi's counsel to "liken the scriptures" (1 Nephi 19:23) unto yourself. Think about how you can personally apply the principles of the passages you are reading. As you do this the Holy Ghost will enlighten your mind with the application.

F. *Restate in your own words.* Stop and restate in your own words what you have read. By doing this you are forced to stop and think about what the passage is truly trying to teach. We know that a person who teaches someone else expands his own learning. Because of this, you may even want to explain to someone else what you have read.

G. *Put your name in the scriptures.* Where possible, mentally insert your own name in the scriptures as you read. This skill adds personal meaning to the scriptures. The following is an example of this: "For behold, I, God, have suffered these things for [your name] that [your name] might not suffer if [your name] would repent; but if [your name] would not repent [your name] must suffer even as I; which suffering caused myself, even God, the greatest of all, to tremble because of pain, and to bleed at every pore, and to suffer both body and spirit" (D&C 19:16–18).

4. *Read and study the conference addresses.* Don't forget that God's most recent word to us can be heard in the latest conference addresses. They are printed in the *Ensign* the month following conference. Elder Harold B. Lee taught: "As the Latter-day Saints go home from this conference, it would be well if they consider seriously the importance of taking with them the report of this conference and let it be the guide to their walk and talk during the next six months. These are the important matters the Lord sees fit to reveal to this people in this day [in this year]." (CR, April 1946, p. 68.)

During the six months between successive confer-ences, then, we should study and ponder the words of the living prophets. The most recent conference ad-dress is God's latest revealed word to us.

7

An Invitation Through Worthy Thoughts

It was the first day of April, and the teachers at Central elementary school had planned to get the jump on the students by playing an April Fools' joke on them. Two of the teachers took all of the desks out of their room and put them in a workroom next door. As the students arrived they scanned the bare room and asked what had happened to their desks.

When the teachers answered with silence or a shrug of their shoulders, the students tried to figure it out themselves. They knew how much space there was in the workroom, and a couple of boys volunteered to check it out. As the boys headed into the workroom, one of the teachers warned them not to go. She teased that there were fumes leaking in the workroom that would make them sick if they breathed them.

It was all a part of the April Fools' fun, but to that classroom of students who heard about the fumes the fun backfired. It wasn't long before several of the students started complaining that they felt sick. They were truly sick from what they believed were fumes leaking in the workroom. The teachers finally told the students that it was all a joke, but this did not make the students feel better immediately. Some still felt sick to their stomachs and others complained of headaches. Several became so overcome by their ailments that they were excused to go home.

By the next day everybody was fine and back to normal. But this innocent April Fools' joke illustrates to us the power of our thoughts. Not only can our thoughts have an effect on our physical well-being but also they can have a profound effect upon our spiritual well-being.

I once received a small package from a friend. As I opened it I found a small note and a "Ding Dong" cupcake. I opened the note and read, "You are what you eat." (I ate the "Ding Dong" anyway). This is not only true for what we eat, but also for what we think. Many of us literally become "Ding Dongs" because of our thoughts. President George Albert Smith described it in this way: "You will be held accountable for your thoughts, because when your life is completed in mortality, it will be the sum of your thoughts." (*Sharing the Gospel with Others,* comp. Preston Nibley [Salt Lake City: Deseret Book Co., 1948], p. 63).

Our feelings, actions, and even sometimes our physical condition are a direct reflection of our thoughts. "Remember, you are today where your thoughts have brought you. You will be tomorrow, and the next day, and every day where your thoughts will take you." (Thorpe B. Isaacson, CR, October 1956, p. 12.)

King Benjamin recognized the influence thoughts have on our eternal destiny. He said:

> And finally, I cannot tell you all the things whereby ye may commit sin; for there are divers ways and means, even so many that I cannot number them. But this much I can tell you, that if ye do not watch yourselves, and your thoughts, and your words, and your deeds, and observe the commandments of God, and continue in the faith of what ye have heard concerning the coming of our Lord, even unto the end of your lives, ye must perish. And now, O man, remember, and perish not. (Mosiah 4:29–30.)

Both Heavenly Father and Satan understand the power that thoughts have to invite the Spirit into or drive it from our lives. Worthy thoughts can have an immediate influence and invite the Spirit to be with us. In contrast, unworthy thoughts can quickly drive the Spirit from us.

Elder Boyd K. Packer described in this way the battle that Satan wages for our thoughts:

> The mind is like a stage. Except when we are asleep the curtain is always up. There is always some act being performed on that stage. It may be a comedy, a tragedy, interesting or dull, good or bad; but always there is some act playing on the stage of the mind.
>
> Have you noticed that without any real intent on your part, in the middle of almost any performance, a shady little thought may creep in from the wings and attract your attention? These delinquent thoughts will try to upstage everybody.
>
> If you permit them to go on, all thoughts of any

virtue will leave the stage. You will be left, because you consented to it, to the influence of unrighteous thoughts.

If you yield to them, they will enact for you on
the stage of your mind anything to the limits of
your toleration. They may enact a theme of bitterness, jealousy, or hatred. It may be vulgar, immoral, even depraved.

When they have the stage, if you let them, they
will devise the most clever persuasions to hold
your attention. They can make it interesting all
right, even convince you that it is innocent—for
they are but thoughts.

What do you do at a time like that, when the
stage of your mind is commandeered by the imps
of unclean thinking?—whether they be the gray
ones that seem almost clean or the filthy ones
which leave no room for doubt.

If you can control your thoughts, you can overcome habits, even degrading personal habits. If
you can learn to master them you will have a
happy life. (CR, October 1973, p. 24.)

The stage of our mind can become so full of evil
that no good can be found in our actions, as was the
case in the days of Noah. "And God saw that the
wickedness of man was great in the earth, and that
every imagination of the thoughts of his heart was only
evil continually" (Genesis 6:5). Satan's goal is to have
this condition exist in all of our minds. He knows that
the Holy Spirit cannot influence our lives when our
thoughts are evil.

The opposite is also true. Heavenly Father knows
that Satan's spirit cannot influence our lives when our
thoughts are virtuous. That is why the Lord gave us the
following instructions with a promise: "Let virtue gar-

nish thy thoughts unceasingly; then shall thy confidence wax strong in the presence of God" (D&C 121:45).

Some actors that Satan likes to place on the stage of the mind and that we sometimes do not recognize as evil are thoughts of worthlessness and despair. Just as filthy thoughts drive the Spirit from us, so do thoughts of worthlessness and despair. Simply by identifying the opposites of these words, we can see that the words are not thoughts from God. When we have thoughts and feelings of worth concerning ourselves and our relationship to Heavenly Father we will feel his Spirit in our lives. Likewise, faith has the same effect, as it gives us hope in the future and God's plan for us.

Our thoughts are the foundation on which our eternal destiny is based. Elder Ezra Taft Benson summed it up when he said: "Thoughts lead to acts, acts lead to habits, habits lead to character—and our character will determine our eternal destiny" (*Ensign,* April 1984, p. 10).

Satan, however, would have us believe that our thoughts are not that important. The very fact that he wants us to believe this lie should be a signal of how important controlled, virtuous thoughts are to having the direction of the Spirit in our lives.

The following are some suggestions for improving our invitation to the Spirit through worthy thoughts.

1. *Be where you should be.* One of the tragic stories in the Old Testament is that of David and Bath-sheba. We read: "And it came to pass, after the year was expired, at the time when kings go forth to battle, that David sent Joab, and his servants with him, and all Israel; and they destroyed the children of Ammon, and besieged Rabbah. But David tarried still at Jerusalem." (2 Samuel 11:1.) We commonly believe that David's

first mistake, leading to his eventual downfall of adultery and murder, was when he let his thoughts dwell on what he had seen as he walked upon the roof of the king's house. This obviously was a wrong decision and was a major factor contributing to his downfall. It appears that the first mistake he made, however, was not being where he should have been. He should have been with his troops in battle, but instead he stayed home.

Often our thoughts are fueled by the environment we are in. "As the thought is father to the deed, exposure can lead to acting out what is nurtured in the mind" (David B. Haight, *Ensign*, November 1984, p. 70). If we are in the right places, are where we are supposed to be, many evil and unworthy thoughts will never enter our mind. In addition, a righteous environment can snuff out many unwanted thoughts as they come to mind.

2. *Forsake the lusts of your eyes.* President Ezra Taft Benson counseled us:

> Consider carefully the words of the prophet Alma to his errant son, Corianton, "Forsake your sins, and go no more after the lusts of your eyes" (Alma 39:9).
>
> "The lusts of your eyes." In our day, what does that expression mean?
>
> Movies, television programs, and video recordings that are both suggestive and lewd.
>
> Magazines and books that are obscene and pornographic.
>
> We counsel you . . . not to pollute your minds with such degrading matter, for the mind through which this filth passes is never the same afterward. Don't see R-rated movies or vulgar videos or par-

ticipate in any entertainment that is immoral, sug-gestive, or pornographic. Don't listen to music that is degrading. (CR, April 1986, p. 58.)

All of the things mentioned above by President Benson have a great impact on our thoughts. If we do not control the things we allow to enter our mind, they will eventually control us. As we feed our minds with the "lusts of the eyes" the Spirit of the Lord will leave us and the spirit of Satan will abound. This spirit will then lead us to do evil deeds that will deny us the eternal happiness which can be ours.

Captain Moroni understood this concept when he asked Pahoran the following question: "Do ye suppose that God will look upon you as guiltless while ye sit still and behold these things? Behold I say unto you, Nay. Now I would that ye should remember that God has said that the inward vessel shall be cleansed first, and then shall the outer vessel be cleansed also." (Alma 60:23.)

3. *Take control.* "If one could look into your heart when you have nothing in particular to do but to live with your thoughts, one could predict your future happiness and successes or your future heartaches and failures" (Milton R. Hunter, CR, April 1963, p. 15).

It is in our hands to determine whether or not the Spirit influences our life. To have the influence of the Spirit we must first take control of our thoughts. Elder Boyd K. Packer stated: "One who can control his thoughts has conquered himself." He then went on to tell the following experience:

When I was about ten years old, we lived in a home surrounded by an orchard. There never seemed to be enough water for the trees. The ditches, always fresh-plowed in the spring, would soon be filled with weeds. One day, in charge of the irrigating turn, I found myself in trouble.

As the water moved down the rows choked with weeds, it would flood in every direction. I raced through the puddles trying to build up the bank. As soon as I had one break patched up, there would be another.

A neighbor came through the orchard. He watched for a moment, and then with a few vigorous strokes of the shovel he cleared the ditch bottom and allowed the water to course through the channel he had made.

"If you want the water to stay in its course, you'll have to make a place for it to go," he said.

I have come to know that thoughts, like water, will stay on course if we make a place for them to go. Otherwise our thoughts follow the course of least resistance, always seeking the lower levels. (CR, October 1973, pp. 23–24.)

As Elder Packer indicated in that same conference address, one excellent way to take control and channel our thoughts properly is to be prepared to replace unworthy thoughts with something else more inviting to the Spirit. A favorite hymn or scripture works beautifully. When a thought that drives the Spirit from us enters our mind, we can quickly sing a song or recite a scripture in our mind. As we work at doing this it will become automatic—when a bad thought enters, the song or scripture will turn on and drive the bad thought from the mind.

Just remember the bottom line: If we do not control our thoughts, Satan will.

8

An Invitation Through Worthy Music

Jared was very excited to turn sixteen. Sixteen meant that he could finally get his driver's licence; but, more important, it also meant that he would be able to get a job. He dreamed about the things he could buy with his own money. His parents had given him some music tapes for Christmas, but he had a long list of tapes he still desired. As soon as he got a job, he knew what his first purchases would be. He would continue to buy tapes until he had a large collection.

Mr. Butler had told him that the moment he turned sixteen he could apply at the Foodmart as a bag boy. The day after his birthday, he filled out the forms and was hired. Jared couldn't remember ever being so excited about something.

After he started the job, he bought himself a few tapes with each pay check. It wasn't long before he had a nice collection. In fact, over a period of time he had purchased well over two thousand dollars' worth of tapes.

As time went on, Jared noticed that his feelings and even his lifestyle were changing. He found himself doing some things he knew were wrong and that he felt uncomfortable about. He was not happy; in fact, he seemed to be depressed most of the time. He had stopped reading the scriptures and going to church. Seminary and Mutual seemed to be a drag and he wanted to stop going, but his parents told him that he had to go if he wanted to drive the car. So he started sluffing Seminary and skipping out on Mutual and then lying to his parents about where he had been.

Instead of hanging out with his friends, Jared was spending more and more time in his bedroom listening to his tapes. His life seemed to be in a downward spiral and he didn't know how to get out of it.

One day when he came home from work there was a note saying that Brother Harrison, the ward executive secretary, had called. Jared returned the call to see what he wanted. Brother Harrison asked Jared if he could meet with the bishop Wednesday night at eight o'clock. Jared told him that would be fine, but wondered what the bishop wanted.

The closer Wednesday night came, the more he didn't want to go. He finally decided to conveniently forget the appointment.

Brother Harrison called the following week and made another appointment. Jared lied to him about why he had missed the first appointment, but there was no way he was going to get out of the next one— Brother Harrison had mentioned the appointment to Jared's mother, and he was going!

As Jared went into Bishop Gordon's office he was very nervous. The bishop, however, put him at ease with a friendly handshake and a warm smile. Jared had always liked Bishop Gordon and was glad he had come. Maybe the bishop could help him get back on top of things and get over the feelings of depression that were overwhelming him.

As they talked about how things were going, Jared was honest and told the bishop how he was really feeling. The more they talked, the clearer it became to Jared that he was no longer feeling the Spirit in his life. In fact, he was feeling an opposite spirit that was not peaceful nor uplifting. As he and the bishop discussed what was going on, the root of the problem hit Jared square in the face. It was the music he was listening to. Now that he thought about it, he had noticed a bad feeling every time he had entered his bedroom. He shook his head as he thought about how stupid he had been.

After he told the bishop what he felt the problem was, Bishop Gordon dropped a bombshell on him. He told Jared that his depressed feelings were not going to go away as long as the tapes were in his home. The bishop suggested getting rid of some of them.

Jared thought about his collection and about how much money was involved. Mentally clicking through each tape, he knew that almost every tape contained unworthy music. How could he discard the more than two thousand dollars he had invested in the tapes? He knew he could not go on feeling and living the way he had the past few months, but did he have the courage to take the first difficult step toward change?

Bishop Gordon could tell that Jared was struggling. He suggested Jared go through the tapes and box up those he felt were driving the Spirit from his life. After he finished boxing them up he was to give the bishop a call. The bishop would then come by and pick up the tapes.

The next day, as hard as it was, Jared went through his collection and ended up putting most of his tapes in the box. Bishop Gordon came by, picked up the tapes, and disposed of them in a nearby garbage bin.

At the time Bishop Gordon picked up the tapes he suggested to Jared that he might want to replace the tapes with others containing music that would bring the Spirit into his life rather than drive it away. Jared followed the advice of his wise bishop and felt an immediate change come into his bedroom and into his life.

Jared's life continued to improve. He returned to full church attendance and daily scripture reading, and spent quality time with good friends. He has since gone on to serve a very successful mission.

Jared's experience demonstrates to us the powerful effect music can have on us for good or bad. Elder Charles W. Nibley affirmed this when he stated: "There is something in the spirit of song . . . an influence . . . and inspirational power . . . that fires the soul in a way that it can't otherwise be touched or fired" (CR, October 1917, p. 75).

I have found that worthy music almost immediately invites the Spirit into our lives. Two of the most sacred occasions of my life involved music. I will never forget them because they were branded on my soul forever by the Holy Spirit.

President Harold B. Lee expressed his feelings concerning music's power to invite the Spirit when he stated: "My experience of a lifetime, and particularly the last thirty-two years as a General Authority, convinces me that the most effective preaching of the gospel is when it is accompanied by beautiful, appropriate music" (CR April 1973, p. 181).

Throughout the scriptures we find reference to the powerful influence music has upon our relationship with our Heavenly Father. Jesus Christ himself stated: "For my soul delighteth in the song of the heart; yea, the song of the righteous is a prayer unto me, and it shall be answered with a blessing upon their heads" (D&C 25:12).

Throughout the Old Testament, reference is made to the use of music to praise God. One such incident took place after the Israelites had successfully crossed the Red Sea on dry ground. At that time they sang a song to the Lord. "Then sang Moses and the children of Israel this song unto the Lord, and spake, saying, I will sing unto the Lord, for he hath triumphed gloriously: the horse and his rider hath he thrown into the sea" (Exodus 15:1). (The words of the song are found in Exodus 15:2–19.)

The Lord counseled the Saints as they crossed the plains: "If thou art merry, praise the Lord with singing, with music, with dancing, and with a prayer of praise and thanksgiving" (D&C 136:28).

Throughout the history of the earth man has recognized the power music has to lift and inspire. David and Solomon used music in times of despair, endeavoring to lift their spirits.

Music has an eternal nature. King Benjamin understood this. "I am about to go down to my grave . . . and my immortal spirit may join the choirs above in singing the praises of a just God" (Mosiah 2:28).

One of the most glorious scriptural accounts of the use of music is found in Luke's account of when angels sang at the birth of Jesus. Music is not something new to us. I am sure that music was an important part of our premortal life and therefore many songs strike a chord with our soul when we hear them.

When my family lived in Florida my wife taught piano lessons, and from time to time she held a recital in our home. Some of the students were from families that were not members of the Church, and at one of the recitals I found myself in the back of a packed room sitting next to the father of one such family. As we were waiting for the recital to start, an unusual thing happened. Hanging on our wall in the front of the room was a plaque with the words "I Am a Child of God" on it. As that father looked at the plaque he repeated the words, "I am a child of God," but he did it to the tune of the song. I have often wondered how he knew the tune to that wonderful song.

My father-in-law was a member of the Episcopal church. When he passed away the funeral was held at his church. His grandchildren sang "I Am a Child of God" as part of the funeral program and many of the members of my father-in-law's church commented on how deeply that beautiful song had touched them. One lady from the church contacted my mother-in-law, who is a member of the Church and asked if she could get a copy of the song so that she could teach it to the children at the Episcopal church. That particular song just seems to strike a chord with Latter-day Saints and other good people alike.

Satan also recognizes the power worthy music has to invite the Spirit. He therefore uses his own brand of music to drive the Spirit from our lives. Ardeth G. Kapp described it in this way: "Music has a very powerful and wonderful influence in establishing feelings and moods that can lift and elevate your thoughts and your actions. But because it is so powerful, it is cleverly used by the adversary to stimulate your thoughts, feelings, and moods, to pollute and poison your mind and cause you to do things you would not otherwise consider doing." (*Ensign,* November 1990, p. 94.)

The following are some suggestions for improving our invitation to the Spirit through the use of worthy music.

1. *In time of trial and sorrow, use worthy music to lift and inspire.* As the time of the Atonement drew near, Jesus and the Twelve sang a hymn at the Last Supper (see Matthew 26:30). John Taylor sang "A Poor Wayfaring Man of Grief" for Joseph Smith prior to the latter's martyrdom. It would be well for us to follow this example when serious trials and difficulties confront us. Music has great power to bring the Spirit to us, giving us the strength to endure the hardships we are called to bear.

Elder Boyd K. Packer related the following:

I have a brother who became a brigadier general in the Air Force. During World War II he was a bomber pilot and took part in some of the most dangerous and desperate raids in Europe. He returned to an assignment in Washington, D.C., about the time I finished pilot training in the same B-24 bombers and was heading for the Pacific. We had a day or two together in Washington before I left for overseas.

We talked of courage and of fear. I asked how he had held himself together in the face of all that he had endured.

He said, "I have a favorite hymn—'Come, Come, Ye Saints,' and when it was desperate, when there was little hope that we would return, I would keep that on my mind and it was as though the engines of the aircraft would sing back to me:

'Come, come, ye saints,
No toil nor labor fear;
But with joy wend your way.
Though hard to you
This journey may appear,
Grace shall be as your day.'"
(*Ensign,* January 1974, p. 28.)

2. *When you sing, sing with the Spirit.* In Paul's epistle to the Corinthians he stated: "I will sing with the spirit, and I will sing with the understanding also" (1 Corinthians 14:15). The words of the hymns teach great gospel lessons. As you sing, pray in your heart for the Spirit and then think of the words of the song and their meaning. As you do so, the Spirit will deliver to your mind spiritual insights that will broaden your understanding of the gospel plan. Some of the greatest lessons we can learn will come as we sing the hymns of the Church.

3. *Surround yourself with worthy music.* The First Presidency of the Church counseled: "Through music, man's ability to express himself extends beyond the limits of the spoken language in both subtlety and power. Music can be used to exalt and inspire or to carry messages of degradation and destruction. It is therefore important that as Latter-day Saints we at all times apply the principles of the gospel and seek the guidance of the Spirit in selecting the music with which we surround ourselves." (Priesthood Bulletin, August 1973.)

We are familiar with the way the pioneers would encircle their camps at night with their wagons as a barrier or protection from harm. The practice of surrounding ourselves with worthy music can protect us just as the wagons protected the pioneers. Elder Boyd K. Packer has taught:

> There is so much wonderful, uplifting music available that we can experience to our advantage. Our people ought to be surrounded by good music of all kinds.
>
> Parents ought to foster good music in the home and cultivate a desire to have their children learn the hymns of inspiration.

The time for music lessons seems to come along when there are so many other expenses for the family with little children. But we encourage parents to include musical training in the lives of their children.

Somehow Andrew and Olive Kimball did, and Spencer learned to play. Somehow Samuel and Louisa Lee managed to do it, and Harold learned to play. And now, as the leaders of the Church assemble for our sacred meetings in the upper room of the temple, we always sing a hymn. At the organ is President Spencer W. Kimball or President Harold B. Lee.

How wonderful is the music instructor who will teach children and youth to play and will acquaint them with good music in their formative years, including the music of worship. To have such music as a part of one's life is a great blessing. (*Ensign,* January 1974, p. 27.)

9

An Invitation Through the Temple

Mike was sixteen and had a mind filled with questions. His greatest question was "Is there really a God?" How he longed for the answer to his question! He had long discussions with his friends, his family, and his seminary teacher. They all suggested that he read the Book of Mormon and then pray fervently for the answer.

One day as Mike was driving and pondering, he went past one of the Church's beautiful temples. As he looked at the temple a powerful, warm feeling came over him, testifying to him that the temple was the house of God.

Mike's experience demonstrates the power the temple has to invite the Spirit into our lives. In Mike's case, just seeing the temple immediately invited the Spirit. There is a special spirit that can be felt when walking on the grounds of the temple. Every year, millions of people visit temple grounds throughout the world. For many, the experience of feeling the Spirit as they walk the grounds encourages further study and investigation. The Spirit is there because the grounds are sacred and holy.

If seeing and entering the grounds brings the Spirit, can you imagine the Spirit that abides within the walls of the temple? Elder Harold B. Lee shared an incident recorded by a temple watchman.

The watchman told about a large group of young men and young women from the Spokane Stake who traveled to the Salt Lake Temple to perform baptisms for the dead. They did baptisms for approximately 750 people. As they came out of the temple the watchman saw one of them, a young girl, go up the steps to the main entrance on the east side. Approaching her, he noticed she was standing facing the door and praying. He waited until she was finished; and as she came down the steps and over to him he saw tears of joy streaming down her face. She said, "This has been the happiest day of my life." (See *Improvement Era,* June 1957, p. 406.)

The Holy Spirit can be felt immediately as we enter the temple. Elder Franklin D. Richards has said: "A temple is a retreat from the vicissitudes of life, a place of prayer and meditation providing an opportunity to receive inner peace, inspiration, guidance, and, frequently, solutions to the problems that vex our daily lives. A temple is a place where . . . the infinite in man, can seek the infinite in God." (*Ensign,* November 1986, p. 71.)

A temple is indeed a house of God. Brigham Young stated: "We build temples because there is not a house on the face of the whole earth that has been reared to God's name, which will in anywise compare with his character, and that He can consistently call His house. . . . He requires his servants to build Him a house that He can come to, and where He can make known His will." (*Journal of Discourses* 10:252.)

Knowing the power that the temple has to invite the Spirit into our lives, Satan does all he can to stop the building of these great edifices. Quoting Brigham Young again:

> Some say, "I do not like to do it, for we never began to build a Temple without the bells of hell beginning to ring." I want to hear them ring again. All the tribes of hell will be on the move, if we uncover the walls of this Temple [Salt Lake]. But what do you think it will amount to? You have all the time seen what it has amounted to. (*Journal of Discourses* 8:355–56.)

> All the angels in heaven are looking at this little handful of people, and stimulating them to the salvation of the human family. So also are the devils in hell looking at this people, too, and trying to overthrow us. (*Journal of Discourses* 18:304.)

> I think there is a work to be done then which the whole world seems determined we shall not do. What is it? To build temples. We never yet commenced to lay the foundation of a temple but what all hell was in arms against us. That is the difficulty now: We have commenced the foundation of this temple. (*Journal of Discourses* 13:329.)

Satan is not only interested in stopping the building of the temples but he also wants to stop us from entering the temple. He will do all he can to discourage us from attending, understanding all too well the spiritual lift the temple can bring into our lives.

Elder Rudger Clawson, who was a member of the Quorum of the Twelve, related an incident told to him by Marriner W. Merrill, president of the Logan Temple (later an Apostle). One morning, President Merrill noticed a great number of people entering the temple grounds. As he wondered who they were, a person he didn't know entered his room.

> Brother Merrill said to him: "Who are you and who are these people who have come up and taken possession of the Temple grounds unannounced?"
>
> The man answered and said: "I am Satan and these are my people."
>
> Brother Merrill then said: "What do you want? Why have you come here?"
>
> Satan replied: "I don't like the work that is going on in this temple and feel that it should be discontinued. Will you stop it?"
>
> Brother Merrill answered and said emphatically, "No, we will not stop it. The work must go on."
>
> "Since you refuse to stop it, I will tell you what I propose to do," the adversary said. "I will take these people, my followers, and distribute them throughout this temple district, and will instruct them to whisper in the ears of people, persuading them not to go to the temple, and thus bring about a cessation of your temple work." Satan then withdrew.
>
> President Merrill, commenting on this strange interview with the Evil One, said that for quite a period of time the spirit of indifference to temple work seemed to take possession of the people and very few came to the House of the Lord. The presumption was that Satan had carried out his threat which caused a temporary lull in Temple work. (Church Section, *Deseret News,* December 12, 1936, vol. 344, no. 61.)

We must always remember and be aware that Satan will exert his influence to turn our thoughts away from the temple. He knows that the temple will provide us with the spiritual strength to withstand his influence. Elder John A. Widtsoe taught:

> In view of this great temple activity, we may well prepare ourselves for opposition. There never yet has been a time in the history of the world when temple work has increased without a corresponding increase in the opposition to it. Some three or four years after the pioneers came to this valley, President Brigham Young said that it was time to begin the building of a temple; and some of the old timers here will probably remember that thousands of the Saints dreaded the command, because they said, 'Just as soon as we lay the cornerstone of the temple, all hell will be turned loose upon us and we will be driven out of the valleys.' President Young thought that was true, but they also would have, if temple work were undertaken, a corresponding increase in power to overcome all evil. Men grow mighty under the results of temple service; women grow strong under it; the community increases in power; until the devil has less influence than he ever had before. The opposition to truth is relatively smaller if the people are engaged actively in the ordinances of the temple. ("Temple Worship," *Utah Genealogical and Historical Magazine,* April 1921, p. 51.)

The following are some suggestions for improving our invitation to the Spirit through the temple.

1. *Leave the world behind when attending the temple.* When we attend the temple, we need to leave the world outside and truly feel the influences of God

through the Spirit. We should approach the experience as if we were entering heaven. President Thomas S. Monson described it in this way: "How far is heaven? It is not very far: in the temples of God, it is right where you are. (*Ensign,* November 1986, p. 99.)

I am very dependent upon my watch and wear it most of the time. There are, however, two places where I like to take my watch off and forget about time and all the demands it makes upon me. One of those places is a summer vacation spot in Alpine, Wyoming, a beautiful piece of God's earth. When I go there I leave behind the phone and other cares of everyday life so that nothing interrupts my time with my family and nature. It is so refreshing to forget the time and enjoy the beauties around me.

Likewise, when I attend the temple I like to remove my watch and enjoy what God has to give me while I am there. It gives me almost the same refreshment that Alpine does but with an added bonus—I feel the powerful influence of the Spirit and the wonderful feeling that I have done something for someone that they cannot do for themselves.

Elder David B. Haight has said:

> The moment we step into the house of the Lord, the atmosphere changes from the worldly to the heavenly, where respite from the normal activities of life is found, and where peace of mind and spirit is received. It is a refuge from the ills of life and a protection from the temptations that are contrary to our spiritual well–being. We are told that "he who doeth the works of righteousness shall receive his reward, even peace in this world, and eternal life in the world to come." (D&C 59:23.) (*Ensign,* November 1990, p. 61.)

2. *Use the temple to receive comfort and revelation when confronted with life's challenges.* Julie Hauwiller related how happy her life was after joining the Church. She had received a lot of joy and satisfaction from serving in the Church and felt she had a strong testimony of the gospel. While watching television one day she saw an anti–Mormon documentary. During the program, she felt an unsettling feeling overshadow her. The feeling lingered on even after the program finished. She said: "The empty, dark feelings I had experienced while watching the show stayed with me. A frightening thought came: what if the Church *isn't* true? In spite of the blessings my Church membership had brought into my life, I was tempted to begin doubting it."

The feeling lingered and threatened to overwhelm her. A few days later, her husband suggested she might find the peace she was looking for at the temple. Even though their closest temple was over six hundred miles away and it would cost a large sum of money to go, Julie decided to make the trip. The visit to the temple brought the desired calming of her spirit.

The peaceful feeling I felt at the temple was wonderful. But I still had questions. Exactly what was I doing there? What was the temple, or for that matter, the Church, really all about?

I went through the first session wondering "Why?" Then, on the next session, I was able to relax and concentrate more on what was happening.

When I least expected it, an answer came. I could feel the presence of a warm, loving spirit that seemed to say, "You're doing the right thing." This calm reassurance instantly wiped away all of my doubts.

I had been confounded by the adversary's propaganda, but I am grateful for that struggle. My testimony of this church is stronger now than ever before. (See *Ensign,* October 1988, pp. 43–44.)

The temple is one of the best places on earth in which to receive help and answers to life's problems. Heavenly Father has all of the answers to all of our questions, and we seem to be able to listen to those answers in the calm atmosphere that is so close to his presence. I personally have received comfort and guidance when I needed it by entering the temple and taking the time to listen for answers.

President Ezra Taft Benson affirmed this when he said: "Prayers are answered, revelation occurs, and instruction by the Spirit takes place in the holy temples of the Lord" (*Ensign,* May 1988, p. 85).

Elder John A. Widtsoe taught:

I believe that the busy person on the farm, in the shop, in the office, or in the household, who has his worries and troubles, can solve his problems better and more quickly in the house of the Lord than anywhere else. If he will . . .[do] the temple work for himself and for his dead, he will confer a mighty blessing upon those who have gone before, and . . . a blessing will come to him, for at the most unexpected moments, in or out of the temple, will come to him, as a revelation, the solution of the problems that vex his life. That is the gift that comes to those who enter the temple properly." ("Temple Worship," *Utah Genealogical and Historical Magazine,* April 1921, pp. 63–64.)

3. *Go to the temple for the right reasons.* As we attend the temple, the type of experience we will have is

directly related to our attitude. I have three reasons why I like to go to the temple and they are the basis for my attitude as I do so.

The first reason is simple: I like how I feel when I enter the temple. The peace and comfort I receive as I feel the Spirit make the visit worthwhile.

Second, I know it is at the temple that the Lord can truly teach and inspire me with the things he wants me to know and understand. This is done through his great instructor the Holy Ghost. Elder F. Enzio Busche commented on the instructions we receive in the temple when he said, "The temple is the only 'university' for men to prepare spiritually for their graduation to eternal life" (*Ensign,* May 1989, p. 71).

Third, temple attendance gives me an opportunity to do something for someone that they cannot do for themselves. It is hard to describe the joy and satisfaction that are felt through the service rendered in the temple in behalf of the dead, especially those of our ancestry.

Elder Victor L. Brown had this to say about our attitude in attending the temple:

> When we go to to the temple because we want to go and not because it is an obligation; when we go with an attitude of worship and a reverence for God and for his son Jesus Christ, and with gratitude for the Savior's sacrifice, when we spend sufficient time to leave the cares of the world outside, wonderful things happen which cannot be described. The Spirit of the Lord distills upon one's soul in these holy houses, truly the most sacred places on earth. A new perception comes into focus of who we are, of what this life is really about, of the opportunities of eternal life, and of our relationship with the Savior. (*Ensign,* November 1989, p. 77.)

10

An Invitation Back

Two days had gone by since Doug had received the invitation from Susan informing him that he was not invited to her party. It had been the most miserable two days of his life. He had spent so many days in anxious anticipation of the party that Susan's cruel invitation had overwhelmed him. The more he thought about it, the more depressed he became. He couldn't figure out what he had done to Susan to cause her to do this to him.

He had been a good friend of Susan's since they were little. In fact, Susan had been his very first friend. He remembered the day they first met. Her dad owned a fruit farm, and Doug and his mother had gone to their fruit stand to buy some cantaloupes. He still remembered how he had chased Susan around the tables, both of them giggling uncontrollably. He had always liked Susan and thought that she liked him. That's why he could not figure out why she would want to hurt him.

As he was lying on his bed, staring at the ceiling and mulling over all of the possible reasons why he had not been invited to "the party of the century," his thoughts were interrupted by his mother calling, "Doug, there's a letter for you. It's from Susan."

Doug ran up the stairs and grabbed the letter from his mother's hand, then ran back down the stairs to his bedroom and locked the door behind him. He quickly opened the letter and read:

Dear Doug:

I'm not quite sure how to say this, but here goes. . . . *I'm sorry!* There is no excuse for what I did. It was wrong and I am sorry. I hope you can forgive me. This is an invitation to be at my party. I hope you will believe what I am about to tell you, because it is true. My party wouldn't be the same without you there. If you can't come I will understand, but I would *really* like to have you there. *Please forgive me.*

A very sorry
Susan

Doug was so excited that he immediately forgave Susan. He really was invited to go to the party! It was only a couple of days away, and he was going to be part of the excitement.

All of us at times reject the Spirit, just as Susan rejected Doug. But, just as Doug was quick to forgive Susan, so is Heavenly Father quick to return the Spirit to our lives if we are willing to take the proper steps. There are none so pleased with our repentance and so willing to forgive us as are Heavenly Father and Jesus.

In fact Jesus has sent his own invitation to us to come back: "Behold, he sendeth an invitation unto all men, for the arms of mercy are extended towards them, and he saith: Repent, and I will receive you" (Alma 5:33).

When we fail to accept this invitation to invite the Spirit into our lives it saddens our Father and the Savior because they know the peace, joy, and comfort that we are refusing. Because of their great love for us they desire only our happiness and joy.

But because of their love for us they have given us agency and will not force the Spirit on us. We must first invite the Spirit into our lives; it is our choice, not theirs. As it states in the book of Revelation:

> Behold, I stand at the door, and knock: if any man hear my voice, and open the door, I will come in to him, and will sup with him, and he with me.
>
> To him that overcometh will I grant to sit with me in my throne, even as I also overcame, and am set down with my Father in his throne.
>
> He that hath an ear, let him hear what the Spirit saith unto the churches. (Revelation 3:20–22.)

As soon as we begin to repent and make a firm decision to open the door and come back to the things that will invite the Spirit, the forces of God start to work in our behalf. The following story is an example of this:

Elder Marshall had been on his mission a little over a year when he was transferred into a new area. After he had been in his new area a few weeks he found that he and his companion were having a hard time obeying the mission rules. Each passing day found them doing things that were a little worse than the day before, until they found themselves violating many of the mission rules. The missionary work almost came to a standstill and Elder Marshall felt a great loss of the Spirit. He had previously felt such a powerful testimony of the gospel that had even grown from his past mission experiences. Now he missed those powerful feelings, and he knew he needed to change. He decided, as the time for transfers approached, that he would pray and ask Heavenly Father to make sure that he was transferred. He asked God to forgive him and to help get him out of the mess he had made.

As the mission president prayed on the morning of the transfers, the Spirit spoke to him, saying that Elder Marshall needed to be transferred. This was a surprise to the mission president, because Elder Marshall was not on the transfer list. Listening to the Spirit, however, the mission president and his assistants reworked the transfers so that Elder Marshall would be transferred.

During the transfer interview, Elder Marshall confessed to the mess that he had made out of the past few months. The mission president acknowledged that mistakes had been made. They had a long discussion about repentance, and Elder Marshall was soon back on track building his testimony and sharing it with investigators. Because Elder Marshall had been willing to open the door, Heavenly Father was able to help lead him back to the Spirit.

On a beautiful, clear winter morning my brother and I flew to Afton, Wyoming. After spending several hours there we prepared for the return trip to Utah. During our stay, however, clouds had developed, and now it was just beginning to snow. We knew that for part of the trip home we would have to use the IFR (Instrument Flight Rule). Simply, this means flying using only the instruments in the plane but no visual reference. We took off planning to head into the clouds, then climb above them as we headed for our destination.

Once we entered the clouds, we had no visual reference to tell us which direction we were going. We were totally dependent on the instruments for guidance. I will never forget that day. The weather was quite nasty as we climbed up through the clouds. Our plane bounced and heaved as we battered our way through the storm.

When the plane finally broke through the top of the clouds the view was breathtaking. As far as we could see below us were beautiful, fluffy white clouds. I felt as if we were in heaven. The sun was bright and the sky was brilliant blue. What had started out as a nasty trip turned into a wonderful flight.

Over the years I have pondered on that particular flight. There we were on the ground in the middle of a snowstorm and then a few minutes later we were in a what seemed like a heavenly state. Such is life. As the storms of life fall upon us, peace and calm often are only a few minutes away.

What brings the peace and calm? It is our willingness to follow the instruments Heavenly Father has given us. His Spirit is always there to direct us through the storms of life, just as on our plane flight the sun had not gone away—it was just hidden from our view.

Heavenly Father and Jesus will never forget us. It is we who forget them. Isaiah wrote: "But Zion said, The Lord hath forsaken me, and my Lord hath forgotten me. Can a woman forget her sucking child, that she should not have compassion on the son of her womb? yea, they may forget, yet will I not forget thee. Behold, I have graven thee upon the palms of my hands; thy walls are continually before me." (Isaiah 49:14–16.)

Satan, of course, does not want us to accept Heavenly Father's invitation to come back. He will do everything in his power to accomplish his goal "that all men might be miserable like unto himself" (2 Nephi 2:27). He would have us believe that we cannot change and improve our lives. He whispers to us that God has forgotten us or doesn't really care. He works subtly to move us away from the influences of the Spirit and then persuades us to believe that it is too hard to return and do those things that will bring and maintain the Spirit in our lives. As Satan tries to wield his influence against God's invitation to us to have the constant companionship of the Spirit, it would be wise to remember the following:

1. *Our spirits know more than our bodies know.* Each spirit dwelt with Father in Heaven and Jesus for a long time before we came to earth and received our bodies. Our bodies are only a few years old. A person's spirit knows and understands far more than his body. It is no wonder, then, that the Holy Ghost speaks to our spirit and Satan speaks to our body. In his great sermon, King Benjamin taught: "For the natural man is an enemy to God, and has been from the fall of Adam, and will be, forever and ever, unless he yields to the enticings of the Holy Spirit, and putteth off the natural man and becometh a saint through the atonement of Christ the Lord, and becometh as a child, submissive, meek, humble, patient, full of love, willing to submit to all things which the Lord seeth fit to inflict upon him, even as a child doth submit to his father" (Mosiah 3:19).

The natural man is ruled by the body and becomes an enemy to the things of the Spirit. If we are to effectively have and maintain the Spirit in our lives we must make the spirit master over the body. Satan desires the opposite: having the body rule the spirit. All of his attacks are aimed at the one goal of having the desires of the body rule over the things of the spirit. We must therefore do those things that will encourage the wiser of the two to be the boss and direct the other.

2. *We must eat every day.* Our spirit needs to be fed spiritual food every day, just as our body needs to be fed physical food. The meals we ate yesterday or last week do us no good today. We can literally starve our spirit if we do not feed it every day. We must daily do those things that invite the Spirit to feed us. Failure to do this may cost us dearly, for the Lord has said: "He that repents not, from him shall be taken even the light which he has received; for my Spirit shall not always strive with man, saith the Lord of Hosts" (D&C 1:33).

3. *Be humble.* I once heard this definition for humility: Humility is to know that there is a God and that you are not him. The best possible response to the important intelligence test is to recognize that God and his prophets and servants are wiser than we are and then follow them. As soon as we think we know more than God and his servants, we become a god to ourselves and the Spirit leaves. Then we are left to ourselves and to Satan's influence. Pride is an enemy to the Spirit and must daily be conquered by humility.

4. *We must control the atmosphere in order for the Spirit to be invited.* "And the Messiah cometh in the fulness of time, that he may redeem the children of men from the fall. And because that they are redeemed from the fall they have become free forever, knowing good from evil; to act for themselves and not to be acted upon." (2 Nephi 2:26.) We must provide for ourselves the right atmosphere, then act upon it in a way that invites and maintains the influence of the Spirit. If we don't, Satan will act upon us. Even worse, we will act in setting an atmosphere that invites the spirit of Satan.

5. *Become spiritually self–reliant.* I grew up on a small farm in rural Utah. We didn't have a lot of money and we therefore relied a great deal on what we produced. We had several fruit trees, a garden, chickens, and other animals. Summer for me was somewhat like a scriptural day of reckoning: a great and dreadful day. It was great because we were out of school. I also loved all of the fresh fruits and vegetables. It was dreadful because of all the weeds to be pulled, irrigation to be handled, and just plain hard work to be done.

In the floor of our barn we had a large pit. In the fall we would put a few bales of straw in the pit and then fill it with the fruits and vegetables we had produced during the summer. For several months, we would live on the potatoes, carrots, and other basic foods that came out of the pit. We even had some watermelons as a treat. I am sure the pit's contents were a great boost to my parents' limited budget as the fall and winter wore on and were especially helpful during those times when money grew tight. Some years we relied more heavily on the pit than others. Always it felt good to know that the food was there if we needed it. My parents always wanted to be self–reliant.

Just as my parents had the foresight to provide and stock a storage area, we should have the foresight to make provision for a spiritual reserve for ourselves. There are bound to be times in life when we will need to draw on extra spiritual strength. If our testimony and our spiritual strength are totally dependent on others, we may not make it through some of the hard times. If, however, we have built for ourselves a spiritual reserve that we can draw upon, we will be able to make it through the narrow passages of life.

Elder Heber C. Kimball, teaching some of the members a lesson, predicted as follows:

Let me say to you, that many of you will see the time when you will have all the trouble, trial and persecution that you can stand, and plenty of opportunities to show that you are true to God and his work. This Church has before it many close places through which it will have to pass before the work of God is crowned with victory. To meet the difficulties that are coming, it will be necessary for you to have a knowledge of the truth of this work for yourselves. The difficulties will be of such a character that the man or woman who does not possess this personal knowledge or witness will fall. If you have not got the testimony, live right and call upon the Lord and cease not till you obtain it. If you do not you will not stand.

Remember these sayings, for many of you will live to see them fulfilled. The time will come when no man nor woman will be able to endure on borrowed light. Each will have to be guided by the light within himself. If you do not have it, how can you stand? (Orson F. Whitney, *Life of Heber C. Kimball* [Salt Lake City: Bookcraft, 1973], pp. 449–50.)

6. *Remember the Spirit's promises and blessings you have been given.* One of the most important requirements of the gospel is to remember. The Lord has given us many things to help us remember him and the covenants we make with him. Elder Spencer W. Kimball stated:

That is the real purpose of the sacrament, to keep us from forgetting, to help us to remember. I suppose there would never be an apostate, there would never be a crime, if people remembered, really remembered, the things they had covenanted at the water's edge or at the sacrament table and in the temple. I suppose that is the reason the Lord asked Adam to offer sacrifices, for no other reason than that he and his posterity would remember— remember the basic things that they had been taught. I guess we as humans are prone to forget. It is easy to forget. Our sorrows, our joys, our concerns, our great problems seem to wane to some extent as time goes on, and there are many lessons that we learn which have a tendency to slip from us. The Nephites forgot. They forgot the days when they felt good. (*SWK Teachings*, pp. 112–13.)

It would be good for us to record the workings of the Spirit in our life; then in times of sorrow, pain, or when our spirits are low we could read and remind ourselves of the goodness of the Spirit in our lives. It is also a good practice to record and remember special blessings that we are given. Priesthood blessings and others, such as our patriarchal blessing, can give us the lift we may desperately need and help us return to the Spirit. In a revelation to Joseph Smith, the Lord stated it simply: "and remember also the promises which were made to you" (D&C 3:5). Elder Spencer W. Kimball related: "I remember a young Navaho boy returning from his mission who was supported largely by a seventies quorum in the Bonneville Stake. I happened to be present the day he made his report and as tears rolled down his face, he said, 'Oh, if I could only remember always just how I feel now.'" (*SWK Teachings*, p. 113.)

7. *Be a tool in God's workshop.* Over the years I have discovered that most repair jobs around the house are relatively simple if you have the right tools. But without those tools, even some simple jobs are al-

most impossible to perform. For that reason I have collected a variety of tools that have saved me a great deal of time and money.

The work in God's kingdom has similar needs, in that as God moves the work along he uses us, his children, as his tools. The tools I own are of no value until I put them to use. They do no one any good just sitting in the shop. The same is true with us. Our value intensifies when God uses us as one of his tools. Many of God's children send an invitation to the Spirit by being a worthy tool used in the hand of God.

My father was not a member of any church. My mother was LDS and encouraged church attendance, but we children were never forced to attend. I went to church quite regularly until I was thirteen. Then I decided I enjoyed my free time at home better than I enjoyed going to church. For about six months I stayed home and played.

One Sunday as I was playing with a friend, I was overcome with a terrible feeling that I was doing the wrong thing. I knew at that moment that I needed to go back to church.

The next Sunday I got out of bed, resolved that I was going back to church. My resolve weakened a bit as I approached the front door of the church; my stomach tied in a knot, and I walked with hesitating steps.

Standing at the door was the new bishop, who was also relatively new to the ward. I didn't know him and I felt sure he didn't know me. As I entered the door the bishop's face lit up, and he put his hand out and said, "Max, it's so good to see you!"

As he spoke those words, a warm feeling came over me and I knew I had done the right thing. I am so grateful that the bishop had taken the time to know my name and my situation. From that time on, I was willing to listen to him and eventually gain a testimony of my own. Bishop Stucki was a fine tool in Heavenly Father's hand that day.

8. *Don't forget grace.* When someone willingly and without reward does something for us that we cannot do for ourselves we have experienced grace. In the gospel there are two kinds of grace. The first and most important type of grace "is [a] divine means of help or strength, given through the bounteous mercy and love of Jesus Christ."

> It is through the grace of the Lord Jesus, made possible by his atoning sacrifice, that mankind will be raised in immortality, every person receiving his body from the grave in a condition of everlasting life. It is likewise through the grace of the Lord that individuals, through faith in the atonement of Jesus Christ and repentance of their sins, receive strength and assistance to do good works that they otherwise would not be able to maintain if left to their own means. This grace is an enabling power that allows men and women to lay hold on eternal life and exaltation after they have expended their own best efforts. (LDS Edition of the Bible, Bible Dictionary, p. 697.)

God's grace goes beyond the effects of the Atonement and salvation. We must recognize that his hand moves in our behalf on many occasions, helping us accomplish many things we would not be able to do on our own. It would be well for us to thank him daily for the grace he bestows upon us.

The second use of grace in the gospel is not divine grace but rather what we might call human grace. I know of a man who needed a heart transplant. The cost of the transplant was one hundred and fifty thousand dollars. Because he was so sick, he could not work. In fact, he had lost his job, and with it any medical benefits. In other words, there was no possible way in which he could get a heart transplant on his own. Several family members, friends, and even people he didn't know raised the money needed for the transplant. This man's life was saved because of the grace of others, including the family that donated their deceased loved one's heart for the transplant.

Throughout our lives we all must learn to be givers and receivers of grace. It may entail the greatest grace of all, which Jesus Christ offers, or the simplest little acts of human kindness. It is through grace, both divine and human, that the Spirit of the Lord can be felt in our lives. It will be by that grace that we eventually return to him, being invited again into his presence.

Index